Unstilled Voices

Unstilled Voices

JAMES and MARTI HEFLEY

HODDER AND STOUGHTON
LONDON SYDNEY AUCKLAND TORONTO

British Library Cataloguing in Publication Data

Hefley, James and Marti
Unstilled Voices

l. Indians of South America–Ecuador
–Missions 2. Aucas
I. Title II. Hefley, Marti
266'.009866   BV2853.E2

ISBN 0 340 272848

*Hodder and Stoughton Editorial Office:
47 Bedford Square, London WC14 3DP*

We reverently dedicate this book to
the memory of the five men who gave
their lives for Christ and the
Aucas on January 8, 1956

Contents

"The Aucas are the most hostile savages known."
Chicago Daily News, January 21, 1956

The Expedition 1

The idea germinated from a conversation between a raw mission recruit and a veteran missionary, at the University of Oklahoma, in the summer of 1950.

"Which tribe in Ecuador is the toughest and most needy?" The intensity in Jim Elliot's piercing blue eyes indicated the seriousness of his inquiry. Dave Cooper, the young man's tutor at the Summer Institute of Linguistics (SIL),* already knew him well enough to realize that the question was typical of his impossibility thinking. Jim was the kind to tackle the steepest and highest mountain. Whatever he did he would do with great gusto.

"That would be the Aucas," Cooper replied. "No outsider has ever been able to live among them. They're in the eastern jungle, out beyond a little town named Arajuno; the town's abandoned by the Shell Oil Company. The Quichuas are their nearest neighbors, and they don't dare go inside Auca territory."

"Really?" Jim responded enthusiastically. "I've been corresponding with Dr. Wilfred Tidmarsh, a Brethren missionary among the Quichuas. He's encouraged me to come to Ecuador, but he hasn't mentioned the Aucas."

"I know Tidmarsh well. He knows about the Aucas.

---

*SIL is a sister organization to the well-known Wycliffe Bible Translators. Although separate entities, they operate under an interlocking directorate and share many objectives.

9

Every missionary in Ecuador does. *Auca* is not actually
the true name of the tribe, though. That's the Quichua
word for 'savage.' Everybody just calls them that because of their reputation."

At Jim's insistence, Cooper offered a quick summary
of what was known about the hostile tribe. They had
fought off Spanish conquistadors in the sixteenth century, killed Jesuit priests who tried to make friendly
contacts, and slaughtered rapacious rubber hunters
who tried to enslave them. More recently, they had
killed a number of Shell Oil Company employees. For
this and other reasons, Shell had left the jungle and
given up prospecting for oil.

"The Aucas have lived up to their reputation; that's
for sure," Cooper concluded.

Jim wanted to know exactly where the Aucas were
located. Cooper indicated on a map an area across the
Andes from Quito, the capital. Auca territory was about
the size and shape of Florida, falling between the Napo
and Villano Rivers, two large streams in the Amazon
tributary system. Like many other Amazonian tribes, he
noted, the Aucas moved around the area, cultivating
small crops in one place for a year or two, then moving
on to fresher land. Numerous times, Shell pilots had
seen clearings with houses. Sometimes they'd seen Indians, but usually, when they flew back over, the
houses were abandoned.

"Have any missionaries tried to go in there?" Jim in-
quired.

"Well, I was in on an attempt a little over a year ago,"
Cooper confided.

"What happened?" Jim asked eagerly.

Cooper explained that he had teamed up with an
adventurer named Rolf Blomberg and a photographer,
Horacio Lopez. Shell loaned them some guns and a

map indicating where pilots had recently spotted some Aucas. They hired a half-dozen reluctant Quichuas as helpers and guides and canoed along the Napo to the mouth of the Arajuno River. From there they crossed by land to the Nushino River, where they camped and built rafts for the float down the smaller stream. All along the way, the Quichuas recounted hair-raising tales of Auca attacks and their cruel ways of killing captives.

The raft trip was slow, and they often felt eyes staring at them from behind jungle undergrowth. They camped again and feasted on fish and game easily taken from the Auca habitat. Their escorts were now noticeably nervous, and at times they all felt that Aucas were watching from the dense jungle

One morning they came upon fresh footprints. The Indians wanted to turn back, but the trio of white men persuaded them to push on. That afternoon, as they were lazily drifting along, six bronze, naked men, wearing only G-strings, suddenly burst out of the jungle and showered spears at them. Everyone but Blomberg dived into the river, including himself, Cooper admitted. The adventurer got off some shots, and the Aucas ran back into the jungle. When the others came up for air, the attackers were gone.

"That was enough for us," Cooper declared. "We turned around and went home."

The challenge stirred Jim's blood. It had been over nineteen hundred years since Jesus gave the Great Commission to "go into all the world." Here was a tribe that had never once heard the gospel of redemption from sin, a tribe that no missionary had ever touched. This was certainly worth praying about.

The year before, Jim had graduated summa cum laude, with a major in Greek, from Wheaton, the queen college of midwestern evangelicalism. There he had been president of the Foreign Missions Fellowship; a champion wrestler with the nickname Rubber Man; a "big man" on campus; an activist in Christian work; a would-be reformer of fundamentalism; and above all, a recruiter for missions, with a long prayer list of prospects. He had been certain of his calling to foreign missions. He had felt drawn to Indian work, perhaps in Ecuador, and had come to SIL to get the linguistic training offered by Wycliffe Bible Translators.

After talking with Cooper, he prayed even harder about Ecuador. The sure conviction that he should go came a few days later as he was reading Exodus 23:20-21 (ASV): "Behold, I send an angel before thee, to keep thee by the way, and to bring thee into the place which I have prepared. Take ye heed before him." He wrote in his journal, "I take this as a leading from God that I should write Tidmarsh telling him that I should come to Ecuador in the will of God."

Jim had vowed to shun any "affairs of this life" that might hinder a missionary, and if a wife and children were hindrances, as his father had once suggested, he was willing to settle for celibacy. Yet he could not forget the bookish yet scintillating Betty Howard, the sister of a former roommate, Dave Howard. Betty was tall and thin, with delicate, light hair, and the remembrance of her filled him with a mixture of joy and longing. An Episcopalian fundamentalist from Philadelphia, where her father edited *The Sunday School Times*, she was also committed to missionary work. Jim had prayed often for God's clear guidance about whether they might have a future together. Now he wondered how she would react to his intention of going to Ecuador.

In September an encouraging letter came from a former college chum, Ed McCully. Ed, a handsome athlete, had been Mr. Everything at Wheaton: senior class president, football and track letterman, one who turned heads as he drove about the campus in his red convertible. Jim and Ed had been a pair of clowns at parties and were practical jokesters, but they also had their serious times and were kindred spirits.

In their senior year, McCully had won the Hearst National Oratory Championship in San Francisco, with a $1,000 first prize. He was welcomed back to Wheaton by over a thousand cheering students. He then joined his classmates for the annual Senior Sneak at a Wisconsin camp on the shore of Lake Michigan. When he arrived, several boys picked him up, put him on their shoulders, and rode him around the camp. Then they walked onto a pier and threw him, fully dressed, into the lake.

Jim had been even less subtle. "Who helped you win that prize, McCully?" he demanded when they were alone. "Who gave you the talent to speak? What are you going to do with it? Use it for yourself or for the glory of the Lord? McCully, you ought to think more about being a missionary." But after graduation, Ed had gone back to Milwaukee and enrolled in Marquette Law School.

Jim smiled as he read Ed's letter: "I have one desire now—to live a life of reckless abandon for the Lord." He took this to mean that Ed had answered a missionary call, and Jim wrote to suggest Ecuador as a possible field.

On a trip home, Jim did some more recruiting. Pete Fleming's family in Seattle had been friends with the Elliots in Portland, Oregon, for years. Pete and Jim had attended Brethren youth camps together. Pete was an athlete and a student leader, serving as student body president of the University of Washington. The

bespectacled young man with thick, black hair and a
quiet wit was earning both his bachelor's and master's
degrees in four and a half years. Before graduating in
1951, he declared his intention of sailing for Ecuador
with Jim the following January.

Jim had hoped that Ed would make the trip a three-
some, but the Milwaukeean had become "hindered" by
a vivacious brunette he had met the previous October
while speaking in her church in Pontiac, Michigan.
Courting mostly by correspondence, Ed persuaded
Marilou Hobolth, the choir leader and youth director of
the church, to say yes, and they were married in June.
The couple planned to follow Jim and Pete to Ecuador,
after the birth of their first child.

Pete hadn't felt free to propose to his fair-haired high
school sweetheart, Olive Ainslie. She promised to write
him while he was gone. Jim left, still praying about
Betty, who now believed that Ecuador was also God's
choice for her.

There were long days of waiting before all six were
serving in Ecuador. Jim and Pete were the first to come.
Then Betty arrived in April 1952 to begin work with the
Colorado tribe on the coastal side of the Andes. Jim was
with Pete among the Quichuas in the eastern Oriente
jungles. Not until after the McCullys arrived with their
son, Steve, did Betty and Jim marry, in October 1953.
The following June, in 1954, Pete returned to the States
to take Olive as his bride.

By 1955 the Elliots, McCullys, and Flemings had established homes in eastern Ecuador, near Auca country,
only a few air minutes apart from one another. Jim and
Betty lived in Shandia, where Jim had built a house and
there was a Plymouth Brethren mission school for local
Quichuas. The joy of their life was adorable, golden-
haired Valerie. Pete and Olive were settled into a little

thatch hut Jim had constructed at Puyupungu. The McCullys, who now had a second son, Mike, were stationed at the old Shell base, Arajuno. Ed had built a house from lumber left behind by the departing oil company. Their home was on the Auca side of the river, and Quichuas were afraid to stay with them after 4 P.M.

Personable, good-humored Nate Saint provided the three families with a lifeline to the outside world. Nate, one of the first members of the newly formed Mission Aviation Fellowship (MAF), regularly dropped by in a little, yellow Piper Cruiser to bring supplies, mail, and an occasional visitor from the outside. When Nate didn't come, Johnny Keenan, the other MAF pilot assigned to Ecuador, did the run to the Brethren outposts.

Nate's home was at Shell Mera, a larger town up the line that had also been abandoned by the oil company. On good terms with Shell personnel, Nate had persuaded the company to deed some of the land and buildings to mission groups. He had personally built a two-story house that served as MAF headquarters and a residence for his delightful blond wife, Marj, and their three young children, Steve, Kathy, and Philip. As if mothering three kids weren't enough, Marj worked as radio operator, bookkeeper, and chief cook and bottle-washer in the unofficial missionary guest house. "The Lord put us here to help you," Nate frequently told missionaries in the area. "Don't ever be bashful about calling on us."

The Saints had been in Ecuador since 1948. While in the army during World War II, a childhood leg infection from osteomyelitis had disqualified Nate from flying military planes, but he managed to get flight training anyway and studied awhile at Wheaton before joining the new mission enterprise dedicated to giving wings to missionaries working in remote areas.

An optimistic sort with crewcut and an infectious grin, Nate was not foolhardy or naive about the dangers of flying over thick jungle where there was no place to land. His concern wasn't just for himself but was also for his missionary passengers, for whom he felt responsibility. One accident and a tribe might be denied the gospel for another decade, until new personnel were trained and ready.

A born tinkerer, Nate was constantly trying to widen the margin of safety in jungle flying. To reduce weight, he stripped the comfortable seat cushions from the Piper. To keep the engine running normally, even if screens and tiny orifices should be plugged with dirt, he devised an alternate fuel system for the single-engine plane. To drop mail and deliver medicine when a landing strip wasn't available, he devised a unique spiral drop to let down small packages on a cord, slowly and accurately, while he circled overhead. To keep himself on schedule in making regular radio reports to Marj, he wore an alarm wristwatch.

Nate and the three Brethren Boys, as the MAF man called Jim, Pete, and Ed, developed close friendships. It was inevitable that they should share with him their concern for the Aucas and pump him for information.

"My sister, Rachel, you know is with Wycliffe," he told them. "She's working with an Auca woman named Dayuma who ran away from the tribe. Rachel's on a hacienda, studying the Auca language with her, right now."

The three could hardly contain their excitement and wanted to know more. "From what Dayuma has told Rachel, the Aucas fear the devil and demons, but they don't worship any god. Spearing is apparently a way of life with them. Dayuma says many of her relatives were killed, and she fled to save her life. Anybody who goes into that tribe will be taking a mighty big risk," Nate cautioned.

During Nate's visits and their overnights at the Saint house, they talked more about the Aucas and ways by which they might be reached. At times they brought up missionaries who had given their lives for the gospel: John and Betty Stam, who had been beheaded by communist guerrillas in China, leaving an infant daughter; Arthur Tylee and his child, who had been beaten to death while his wife was left for dead, by Nhambiquara Indians in Brazil; five men with the New Tribes Mission, who had been slain about a decade before while trying to reach the wild Ayores in Bolivia.

"The way I see it," Nate said, "we ought to be willing to die. In the military, we were taught that to obtain our objectives we had to be willing to be expendable. Missionaries must face that same expendability." The Brethren trio and their wives felt the same way. Ed and Marilou were already facing that expendability by living at Arajuno on the very edge of Auca territory, hoping that giving the Aucas the opportunity to observe them and their children would bring about a friendly contact.

Monday morning, September 19, 1955, Nate dropped off supplies at the McCullys on his weekly run. It was one of those bright jungle days when there was not a threatening thundercloud in the sky. He habitually flew around Auca territory, just in case he had to make a forced landing, but this day he asked Ed, "How'd you like to go looking for your neighbors?"

Ed leaped at the idea, and within half an hour they were buzzing over the vast, unexplored area, searching for Auca clearings. They had about used up the gas available for this reconnaissance flight when they saw a bald spot in the jungle. Nate came in lower. It was a clearing. Within the immediate area, they found about fifteen clearings and some houses. "It was an exciting old time, a time we'd waited for," Nate wrote in his journal.

Ten days later, Nate and Pete Fleming spotted another cluster of clearings and several jungle houses: "Only fifteen minutes (flying time) from Ed's place," Nate wrote exultantly.

October 1, Nate, Ed, Jim, and Johnny Keenan (the other MAF pilot in Ecuador) sipped cocoa over a map of the Oriente that was spread on the Saints' living room floor. They talked about how a contact might be made by locating an Auca clearing, then dropping gifts and talking through a loudspeaker to build up trust. Nate had recently assisted a Gospel Missionary Union missionary, Roger Youderian, in dispelling the fears of the lesser-known Atshuara Indians in this way.

They all agreed that any operation to contact the Aucas should be kept secret. If it became known, they'd be swarmed by journalists, anthropologists, and other outsiders wanting to intrude on the project. If a contact was made, the outsiders might endanger the lives of missionaries and would probably frighten the Aucas back into the jungle. The door of hope might be slammed shut for decades.

Betty Elliot had been listening. "It seems to me it would only be fair to tell Rachel about it," she insisted. "After all, she is already working with that Auca woman."

Nate pointed out that Rachel would probably tell her field administrators. They wanted as few people as possible to know because of fear of a news leak, which was what they wanted most to avoid.

So the decision was made to keep the operation secret from Rachel. Still, they needed to learn some of the

Auca language if they were to communicate from the plane. "I've been over to that hacienda and met Dayuma," Jim mentioned. "I could visit her again and get some helpful words and phrases from her. I wouldn't have to tell Rachel about our plans."

The others thought this was wise, and around midnight they committed themselves to the operation and began making concrete plans. Jim and Ed would fly with Nate over Auca territory as their time permitted. Johnny would serve as backup pilot and be available in case a rescue was needed. After locating an inhabited clearing, they would make weekly gift drops before attempting physical contact.

October 8, Nate and Ed flew over a large longhouse and three smaller thatch dwellings set back from a small river. Skillfully, Nate lowered a small aluminum kettle decorated with colored streamers. The kettle contained brightly colored buttons and a small sack of rock salt. Dayuma had said her people had no salt of their own. The kettle plunked on the beach, directly before a path leading up to the big house, and Nate pulled the line free. "There was our messenger of goodwill, love, and faith, 2,000 feet below, on the sandbar," he recorded in his journal. "In a sense we had delivered the first Gospel message by sign language, to people who were a quarter of a mile away vertically, fifty miles horizontally, and continents and wide seas away psychologically."

They saw no one that day, but when Ed and Nate flew back ten days later, the kettle was gone. Upstream, they found three other dwellings on the river and sighted three or four canoes tied up to the bank in front of a large house. They circled, and Nate eased down a machete while Ed watched through binoculars. The gift was partway down when he yelled to Nate, "There's an

Auca!" Then, "Two more!" A moment later the machete hit the water, followed by the splash of a diver going for it. Others came out of the house until Ed counted a half-dozen men examining the prize. He and Nate flew back elated. They hadn't counted on seeing Aucas nearly so soon.

Over the next three weeks, they located two other houses in the scattered settlement they called Terminal City. They dropped an assortment of treasures, including clothing, and saw Aucas every time. Meanwhile, Jim visited the hacienda and talked with Dayuma, and jotted down helpful Auca phrases on three-by-five note cards. He, Ed, and Nate practiced the phrases, and for the next overflight Nate took along a small, hand-held, electronic megaphone. As they neared the inhabited place, Jim shouted in his best Auca, "I like you! I am your friend! I like you!" A man cupped his hands as if he was answering back. He and others prancing around in the clearing beside the stream did not seem afraid of the plane at all. Some wore the clothes that had been previously dropped.

On the fifth trip, Ed called through the speaker, "We like you! We have come to visit." Then he leaned out the window and extended both hands. Three Aucas responded by reaching up to him.

On another overflight, Aucas on the ground pulled a pot off the line and tied something on. Nate reeled in a headband of woven feathers. "A real answer to prayer; another sign to proceed," Ed noted in his diary.

Jim took the next run with Nate. They flew over the fourth house and saw two men perched on top of a high platform. They dropped an axhead and plastic combs and flew on to house number three. Jim spotted a man wearing a gift shirt and pitched down a pair of pants, then a machete with a pair of shorts attached. They moved back to number four and dropped a kettle in a stiff wind. Here Jim saw an old man waving with both arms, as if saying, "Come down to us."

"Lord, send me soon to the Aucas!" Jim wrote in recalling the scene.

The three kept their wives and the Flemings up-to-date on the progress. Pete still had not committed himself to the project but was praying for God's will. His concern for the Aucas had not diminished, but he also felt an obligation to Olive. She had only been in Ecuador a year, and nine months of that time had been spent in Quito, studying Spanish. During this year, she had suffered two miscarriages, and Pete worried how she would fare if anything happened to him. But this was not his main reason for hesitating. He, Jim, and Ed were among a few missionary men who spoke the language of the jungle Quichuas. It did not seem wise for all of them to take the risk.

Jim, Ed, and Nate figured that pretty soon they would be going in to meet the Aucas. They discussed what they should do if Pete decided not to join in. "I think that even if Pete does help us, we need another, more experienced missionary, too," Nate recommended.

"You know everybody in this area. Whom would you suggest?" Jim asked.

"Rog Youderian might be the one. I know him well. He was raised on a Montana ranch, trained as a paratrooper in the war, and has already established a contact among the Atshuaras."

Jim and Ed knew that Rog was past thirty and thought a younger man might be best.

"I still like Rog," Nate countered. "He really has a

sense of urgency about what the Lord wants us to do."

The Brethren Boys then agreed that "if Roger wants in, we're all for him."

Roger and his dedicated wife, Barbara, were with the Gospel Missionary Union, which had been in Ecuador for over half-a century. He had been partly crippled by polio as a child and by sheer grit had won an athletic scholarship to Montana State College. During the war, he had jumped in the Battle of the Bulge and was decorated for bravery in action.

Unknown to the eager trio, Roger was just emerging from a spiritual depression. He had broken through to the Atshuaras, but he had won no converts. He felt himself a failure and was thinking of taking Barbara and their two children home—the first time he had ever considered turning his back on anything.

Nate found Roger in Shell Mera, nailing down sheets of aluminum on the roof of the new HCJB Vozandes Mission Hospital being built on some land obtained from Shell. He told Rog about the project and explained that they would probably try to land on a beach. "I don't want to keep the plane out in that area overnight," he said. "On the other hand, I don't want to leave Ed and Jim alone that close to the Aucas."

"Sure, I'll help you," Rog said immediately, without bothering to tell Nate of his inner struggles. He returned home to tell Barbara, confident that she would not object inasmuch as he had been away on dangerous excursions before. A few days later he wrote in his diary, "I will die to self . . . I will be alive unto God."

Nate wrote, after talking with Rog, "He knows the importance of unswerving conformity to the will of his Captain. Obedience is not a momentary option; it is a diecast decision made beforehand."

The flights continued through November and into

December. When Nate swooped down to treetop level, no spears were hurled. Once he passed so low that two men on the platform at house number four ducked. On another flight, the missionaries glimpsed a crude model plane the Aucas had left on a roof. Another time a boy tried to climb the drop line to the plane.

The little river had no beaches long enough to land on. The larger Curaray River was not far from Terminal City, and Nate began looking there. They had decided that if no site could be found, Jim and Betty would canoe in to make a land contact.

December 10, 1955, Nate sighted a 200-yard-long beach on the Curaray, about four and a half miles from the homes. Twice he simulated a landing, putting the wheels down lightly, then pulling up. He termed the surface of Palm Beach "smooth as a gravel runway . . . ideal, except for vulnerability to flooding."

They firmed up final plans. Nate would fly his cohorts in one at a time with supplies that included a prefab tree house with aluminum for a roof. He would take one of them over Terminal City daily to invite the Indians to meet them on the beach. They set launch day immediately after New Year's, as soon as the weather allowed.

Marilou McCully was seven months pregnant. But in mid-December, Ed felt it was all right to leave her at Arajuno while he helped with a Bible conference at Pete's and Olive's station in Puyupungu. He persuaded some trusted Christian Quichuas to stay as guards while he was gone. On a pole outside the house, he perched a model plane as an identification symbol to any neighbor who might come visiting.

One morning, as day was breaking, Fermin, one of the Quichua guards, slipped from his post in the schoolhouse to answer the call of nature. Nearing the pole at the end of the path, he spotted a naked man holding a spear. The Auca saw him and dashed back into the jungle.

The Quichua pounded on Marilou's door, shouting, "Auca! Auca!" She hurried out and ran down the path as quickly as her pregnant body would move, calling, *"Biti miti punimupa."* (I like you. I am your friend.) The Quichua ran after her, yelling in his language, "Crazy! Crazy! They'll kill you." When he caught up to Marilou, she was staring at a fresh, bare footprint and still calling, "I like you." But the Auca had vanished.

Through the rest of the month the five couples discussed every possible safety measure. Pete still had not decided if he should take part in the contact, but he couldn't help but be swept up in the excitement as the weekly flights increased the confidence of the men. They were optimistic, but cautious. They planned to carry concealed pistols—to be shown only as a threat and fired in the air if Aucas should advance on them menacingly. Regular radio contacts would be kept with Marj, as Nate always did when away from home. During daylight hours, they would patrol the beach, shouting Auca phrases. At night they were to withdraw into the tree house, leaving a gasoline lamp burning at the foot of the tree.

December 23, Nate and Jim flew over the houses in Terminal City again and counted thirteen Indians. One held up an object as the missionaries dropped a net containing a flashlight, a pair of pants, white cloth, and a few trinkets. When they retrieved the net, it was loaded with a potpourri of exchanges including cooked fish, peanuts, manioc, smoked monkey tail, and a live parrot. It was more encouragement to make their holiday truly festive.

The Elliots and Flemings celebrated Christmas with

the McCullys, at Arajuno. The Youderians and Saints stayed home with their children. On his little typewriter, Nate had already pecked out the reason for the Auca venture: "As we have a high old time this Christmas, may we who know Christ hear the cry of the damned as they hurtle headlong into the Christless night, without ever a chance. As we weigh the future and seek the will of God, may we be as moved with compassion as our Lord."

Between Christmas and New Year's Day, the couples gathered at Shandia to fine-tune their plans. The decision had been made that all three Brethren Boys should go. The five wives talked candidly about the possibility of becoming widows. They were expecting a great victory but were realistic in appraising the risks. They knew their husbands were willing to die in obedience to what they felt was God's command. The willingness of the wives to support their decision was part of that obedience.

New Year's Day 1956, Nate flew Marj and their children back to Shell Mera, where she would be on duty in the nook across from their kitchen that served as their radio room. Olive went along to keep Marj company. Betty stayed at Shandia. Rachel Saint joined her there so she would not be alone while Jim was on "a trip." Rachel still did not know what was going on. Barbara would stay with Marilou.

In their bedroom that evening, Marj watched Nate pack his suitcase. She could see the excitement and anticipation written across his face. "Tomorrow's the big day!" he exclaimed. "We'll need plenty of prayer."

"I'll be praying here," Marj promised. "I'm so happy that the time has come for you fellows to go meet the Aucas."

The next morning Nate ate his usual early breakfast,

kissed Marj and their three sleepy children good-bye, and taxied the yellow Piper across the road that ran beside their house and onto the long, parallel runway. As was their custom, Marj came out into the yard to wave good-bye. She and Kathy and Steve stood on the mound of a hill in the side yard to watch Nate take off. They saw him wave back, then he revved the engine one last time, and minutes later, the Piper was only a speck in the sky.

A quarter hour later, Nate landed in Arajuno, where the other men were already gathered. After a quick cup of Marilou's coffee, they huddled in prayer and sang a much-loved hymn:

We rest on Thee, our Shield and our Defender,
Thine is the battle, Thine shall be the praise
When passing through the gates of pearly splendor
Victors, we rest with Thee through endless days.

Nate dropped Ed on the first landing. Then he circled around, saluted his solitary friend on the beach, and zipped back to Arajuno for Roger and Jim.

Roger had become so close to Jim and Ed in the final planning that Nate referred to them as the three musketeers. He left the jubilant friends clearing debris from the beach and hurried back for their equipment. It took three more flights in the tiny plane to bring in the radio, prefab tree house, food, tools, and other gear. Pete remained at Arajuno, acting as baggage agent and helping Nate load at that end. After his final landing, Nate flew over Terminal City, calling to the Aucas, "We are your friends. Come tomorrow to the Curaray." Then he headed back to Arajuno for the night.

The next morning on their way to the beach, Nate and Pete flew back over Terminal City. They called again and noted a definite thinning of the population below. When they landed at Palm Beach, they discovered that Ed, Jim, and Rog had completed the house, but the radio transmitter was not functioning. Nate found a loose connection in the microphone and was greatly relieved to reach Marj in Shell Mera. Nate and Pete flew out again that evening because Nate didn't want to risk keeping the plane on the beach overnight.

Thursday morning, Nate and Pete saw only a few Aucas around the houses. Slipping over to the Curaray, Nate flew low over a line of smaller beaches below the campsite and sighted unmistakable footprints. That day on the beach, they all felt they were being watched. On another pass over Terminal City, Nate and Pete saw an Auca kneeling on the platform, pointing toward the campsite with both hands. They returned to Palm Beach, glided low, and shouted this information, then headed back to Arajuno, where Marilou and Barbara were holding down the fort.

They radioed the day's news to Marj and Olive at Shell Mera. Anxiety was building among all of them as time passed and no Aucas came visiting. Before slipping into bed at Arajuno, Nate scribbled in his journal, "May we see them soon."

Eleven-fifteen in the morning, the five intrepid pioneers were on the beach. Nate and Pete hunkered in a little cooking shelter. Ed stood a few yards upriver, Roger in the center, Jim a short way downstream, all calling in Auca, "We like you." "We've come to visit." "We are your friends."

Suddenly a strong, masculine voice answered Ed from across the river. Seconds later a girl about sixteen, an older woman, and a man about thirty, all naked except for strings about waists and thighs and wooden plugs in their earlobes, stepped into the clear. This was the moment for which the men had waited. "Welcome!

Welcome!" Jim shouted, wading across to grasp their hands and lead them to the camp.

The beaming missionaries passed out gifts: paring knives, a machete, and a model airplane. They snapped pictures of their visitors, doused "George" (the man) with insect repellent, and showed "Delilah" (the girl) and the older woman pictures in *Time*. None of the visitors showed any fear.

That afternoon, Nate flew "George" over Terminal City. The Auca yelled gleefully to his people. When they landed back on the beach, he jumped out, clapping his hands in apparent delight. The five men lifted their faces and gave thanks to God. They hoped the Aucas would understand they were talking to God.

All continued to go well. Nate and Pete took off in the late afternoon for Arajuno. Nate had already radioed the good news to Marj. Now he and Pete could give the wives at Arajuno the details.

After they left, "Delilah" walked off, with "George" following her into the bush. The older woman hung around until Ed, Roger, and Jim left her by a fire and climbed into the tree house to sleep. The next morning she was gone, but the embers from the fire still glowed.

Saturday morning, nobody showed up. Jim became impatient and threatened to walk over to the houses. Caution kept him back, although he did walk a distance into the jungle on a small trail running back from the tree house.

Sunday morning, Nate and Pete flew over the houses, with Nate calling, "Come! Come!" On a second run they saw "George" and a bunch of men.

They reported this to the men on the beach, taking along Marilou's gift of blueberry muffins and home-made ice cream. Then Nate went up alone and spotted a band of naked Indians coming along the trail. Touching down, he shouted to his colleagues, "They're on the way!"

Nate called Marj exactly at 12:30 P.M., as he had been doing every day. Using the secret code words, he reported "a commission of ten" enroute from Terminal City. "Pray for us," he concluded. "Will be back in touch at four-thirty. Over and out."

The Impact 2

In the house that Nate built, the clock hands crawled agonizingly slowly for Marj and Olive. At 4:30 P.M., Marj sat anxiously by the radio, with Olive huddling nearby. Marilou and Barbara were listening at Arajuno.

Not a sound. Nothing. A minute dragged by . . . two . . . five. In eight years of jungle flying, Nate had never missed a sked (scheduled radio contact).

A little after sundown, Dr. Art Johnston, one of the staff doctors at the new Hospital Vozandes in Shell Mera, stopped by on a routine errand. He saw Marj sitting with her head down on the desk before the radio that was still on. "Something wrong?" he asked kindly.

Marj looked up and tried not to sound frightened. "Nate didn't keep his four-thirty sked. He's never missed before. I, well, I might as well tell you that he, Jim Elliot, Ed McCully, Pete Fleming, and Rog Youderian are on a beach out in Auca country." She poured out the whole story to the surprised medic, requesting, "Please keep this quiet. We wouldn't want to upset anyone unnecessarily." Dr. Johnston promised he would and asked to be kept informed.

At Arajuno, where Nate and Pete were supposed to fly in for the night, Marilou and Barbara had kept busy. Marilou prepared more food for Nate to take out in the morning, while Barbara played Bible school with the four children in Stevie McCully's bedroom. When four-thirty passed with no word, Barbara shrugged her shoulders and reassured Marilou, "Rog has been out many times without calling in. Don't worry, he always comes back. They are probably just busy entertaining their guests." But, as the sun dropped lower and there was no further news, they walked out to the runway to watch and listen for the plane that never came.

The long, restless night finally passed for the young wives. Johnny Keenan had been informed of Nate's failure to call, and at first light he was ready to fly over Palm Beach and have a look. "I'd like to go with you," Barbara requested. "If you don't mind keeping Bethie and Jerry?" she asked Marilou. Marilou quickly nodded. After a moment's hesitation, Johnny realized that the somber, determined woman standing before him would not panic, no matter what they discovered. "OK," he agreed, "two sets of eyes can see twice as much."

Peering down through breaks in the ground fog, Johnny found the beach that Nate had pointed out to him some weeks before. He made a low sweep, and they saw the skeleton of the Piper. "It looks as if it's been attacked by a wild animal," he exclaimed. Through his window, Johnny was pretty sure he saw a body downstream, but he said nothing to Barbara or to Marj when he reported the plane had been damaged. Marilou was listening at Arajuno.

While Johnny and Barbara were still in the air, Marj radioed Betty, who had remained in Shandia with Rachel. Rachel overheard Marj say that Johnny Keenan was flying over the Curaray River at dawn. Nobody flew to that part of the jungle unless there was trouble. Then she heard Marj report that the plane was stripped of its fabric. "Aucas!" Rachel reacted instantly, for the first time realizing what had been going on.

For Betty, this was the first she had heard since noon

the day before, when Nate had called in the last time. Isaiah 43:2 (ASV) came to her: "When thou passest through the waters, I will be with thee; and through the rivers, they shall not overflow thee." With this confidence, she went on to teach her Quichua girls' literacy class.

Larry Montgomery, a Wycliffe pilot, happened to be in Shell and stopped by the Saints' house. Marj and Olive told him about the stripped plane. Larry was a reserve officer in the USAF and knew that General William K. Harrison, commander in chief of the United States Caribbean command, was in Panama. Montgomery immediately phoned Wycliffe's Don Johnson in Quito and requested that Johnson send General Harrison a telegram advising him of the situation.

General Harrison, an evangelical believer, was a friend of the Elliot family and had visited Jim and Betty at Shandia. Pete and Olive had visited in his home shortly after their marriage. He immediately arranged with the Ecuadorian air force for a joint air search and rescue mission.

Gloom thickened among the wives and their missionary friends. Monday evening, Frank Drown, Roger's close friend and veteran missionary to the head-hunting Jivaro Indians, started recruiting a ground-search party. The missionaries would go overland, as Dave Cooper's party had done, in hopes of meeting the five fellows trying to come out.

Secrecy was no longer important. The missionaries realized that news of the rescue efforts would soon get out and they would be besieged by reporters. They decided that the wisest policy would be to have the international missionary radio station, HCJB in Quito, broadcast the full story on progress of the search. That evening, people around the world heard over HCJB's popular "Back Home Hour" that five American missionaries were missing in Auca territory. HCJB promised to keep listeners informed and asked them to pray.

The news from HCJB beat the telegrams sent to notify the parents of the missing men. Monday night, Marilou McCully's mother heard the broadcast at home in Pontiac, Michigan. She immediately called Ed's parents in Milwaukee. When the McCullys recovered from the shock, they asked their closest friends over for a prayer meeting. It was that way from Philadelphia to Seattle. Parents, brothers and sisters, in-laws, scores of relatives, friends, and total strangers joined in an outpouring of prayer. Prayer meetings also sprang up on many Christian college campuses, in the offices of Christian agencies, and in untold numbers of churches and neighborhoods. Perhaps at no time in history were so many people praying for one group of missionaries.

The announcement that five missionaries were missing came during the traditional news lull after the winter holidays, when little was happening. The press was looking for a big story. The search for the five missionaries was it.

FEAR SAVAGES KILL FIVE MISSIONARIES shouted the front page of the *Chicago Daily News*. Hundreds of other newspapers in the United States and abroad gave the story big play. The television and radio networks gave special bulletins. Several times a day, NBC broadcast live reports from HCJB cofounder Clarence Jones in Quito. Millions of listeners heard his first broadcast on Tuesday:

Yesterday the Voice of the Andes was notified that five missionaries had been out of contact with their base for over twenty-four hours. It was reported that the missionaries' plane had been spotted from the air. There have been no signs of life around the plane. The United States Air Force dispatched one of its Albatross rescue planes and crews from Panama this morning. The Ecuadorian Air Force is also cooperating and some twenty soldiers have been flown in by them. Tomorrow, two United States Air Force C-47 planes will fly from Panama to Shell Mera. One will carry an H-13 helicopter; the other a supporting rescue crew. This is Clarence Jones, reporting from NBC, in Quito.

Time-Life had already been considering a story on Nate and his unique spiral drop. When Jerry Hannifin, *Time-Life's* aviation correspondent, heard of the search, he immediately urged his superiors to "get someone down there." *Life* editors dispatched top photographer Cornell Capa to Ecuador.

General Harrison had a strategy room in a secret, highly classified area called the Tunnel at the United States base in Panama. Here, on a map spread out across a central table, he followed the advance of the rescue planes.

The ground search party assembled in Arajuno on Tuesday. Seven missionaries, all close friends of the missing men, all men in their twenties and thirties and with young families, volunteered. Besides Frank Drown, the leader, they included Dr. Art Johnston, Dee Short, Morrie Fuller, Don Johnson, Bub Borman, and Jack Shalanko. None had known of the secret mission. They were joined by thirteen Ecuadorian soldiers and Indian carriers, also volunteers. All knew they might not come back alive.

Tuesday night an Ecuadorian airline pilot came to Marj Saint's house to say he had just flown over the area and had seen a large fire on the Curaray. That he saw no smoke indicated it might be a gasoline fire or a signal flare. Marj knew Nate carried signal flares as part of his emergency equipment and took heart. Another pilot reported having sighted two men waving flags on a river beach in the area where the five had gone. ALIVE IN JUNGLE headlined one newspaper that picked up the dispatch from Associated Press. Hopes rose; the men might be all right.

There were so many rumors and unverified stories flying around that Abe Van Der Puy, field director of the World Radio Missionary Fellowship, came from HCJB in Quito to bang out press releases in the Saints' house. Wednesday, Abe reported that Johnny Keenan had definitely sighted a body about a quarter mile downriver from the denuded plane. The ground rescue team, he said, had now departed Arajuno, and the two USAF C-47s had flown in from Panama carrying the dismantled helicopter. HCJB carried this news to the praying friends and relatives at home.

Thursday morning, the missionary ground crew canoed into Auca territory and met Quichuas paddling up the Curaray River from the opposite direction. They were Christians, friends of Ed McCully, who had overcome their terror of the Aucas to search for Ed and his companions. With stoic faces but sad eyes, they displayed Ed's watch and told of finding his body. They were taking the watch to Marilou.

That afternoon the USAF helicopter fluttered over Palm Beach. The crew counted four partially submerged bodies at intervals along the river. FOUR MISSIONARIES REPORTED KILLED, read the headlines in the newspapers. The lack of details kept alive the feeling of suspense that had gripped the millions who had been following the drama all week. Also, there was the thought, for the parents: *Four bodies. Maybe, just maybe, our boy is still alive.*

Friday morning, the missionary search party came to a tree that had been chopped down. They figured the five had cut it for a landing approach. The beach must be just ahead. Suddenly a Quichua yelled, "Airplane! Airplane!"

"Lord," Frank Drown groaned, "give me grace and strength."

They beached the canoes and ran to the plane. The fiber had been stripped from it, the seats cut. Two climbed into the tree house and found only the radio generator left. Everything else had been thrown into the river.

Frank waded into the water and retrieved Nate's camera, an old sock, and a towel. Another of the missionaries pulled up a shovel. Another got Roger's camera. Others dragged aluminum sheeting to the beach.

The wind was rising, the sky darkening. A storm was imminent. They heard a roar and looked up to see the helicopter. The chopper moved across the water and hovered over a log. Morrie Fuller swam across and saw the body. He reached down and attached a cord to pull it to the beach. It was hardly more than a skeleton loosely covered by clothing.

Following the chopper, the ground team located a second victim two hundred yards downstream; a third, three hundred yards away; and a fourth, a half mile below camp. They presumed that Ed's body, which the Quichuas had found, had been washed away.

When the four bodies were on the beach, Art Johnston, Frank Drown, and Jack Shalanko pulled personal belongings from pockets and identified each one. The physical features were unrecognizable.

The missionaries gently laid the forms on the aluminum strips that the five had used for the roof of their tree house. Six Quichuas carried the strips to a grave on high ground, in the shadow of the tree house, that had been hastily dug with the shovel.

As they were lowering the remains into the shallow hole, the sky exploded in a fury of wind and water. At that moment the helicopter returned, coming in low and fast. Cornell Capa, the photographer-correspondent from *Life*, leaped onto the sand, snapping pictures in the gathering darkness.

Sheets of rain whipped around the missionaries, huddled around the grave. It became as dark as the inside of a tunnel. Lightning and thunder cracked, and the ground literally shook under them. Each one said later that he had felt the power of Satan as never before. But, as Don Johnson recalled, "We knew God was going to honor the sacrifice of our brothers, although we had no idea to what extent."

Fatigued to a razor's edge, the missionaries were almost overcome with anguish. "Dear Lord," Frank Drown croaked over the fresh earth, "watch over the bodies of these, our dear loved ones, until the resurrection morning. May these bodies bring forth fruit, someday, in the salvation of lost Indians."

As the raindrops mingled with their tears, the seven missionaries sloshed back to the beach, where the soldiers had kept guard, fingers on triggers, ready to shoot at the slightest suspicious movement. The helicopter flailed the air and took off, leaving Cornell Capa to accompany the missionaries part of the way back. He spent that night on a cold riverbank with them, with the heavily armed soldiers standing watch. The next day, Capa was picked up by the helicopter and flown back to Shell Mera.

Saturday morning, one of the big USAF C-47 cargo

planes came to take the widows for an overflight of the gravesite. The indefatigable Capa climbed aboard, with his camera, to join the widows on the memorable flight. A few minutes later, the pilot cut speed and began lowering the lumbering hulk toward the river.

The widows knelt on the floor of the plane and pressed their faces to the windows. There was the slash of sand off to the side; the stripped Piper; on the muddy bank was the spot of earth where the grave had been hastily filled in. "That's the most beautiful little cemetery in the world," Marj whispered.

The plane turned and arched up over the jungle where the dwellers of the forest remained imprisoned in their isolation and hostility, apart from those who would bring the message of release. Capa slipped among the women and quietly listened to their reflections. "We knew the risk," he heard Marilou McCully say. "We knew the Lord led. These were Indians who had never heard." Then Betty Elliot: "They died because they were obedient."

Capa had seen death and agony many times before. These women were startlingly serene. "I have such a sense of the presence of God, a feeling that this is His will," Barbara Youderian said. "I keep thinking, He's guided us this far. He will guide us forever."

Olive, the youngest of them all, who had no child of her beloved to cherish, quoted the Scriptures from which she had earlier taken comfort: "For we know that if our earthly house of this tabernacle were dissolved, we have a building of God, an house not made with hands, eternal in the heavens. . . . Therefore we are always confident, knowing that, whilst we are at home in the body, we are absent from the Lord" (2 Corinthians 5:1, 6, KJV).

There was never any thought of bringing the bodies

out, but a memorial service was planned for the next
morning. Nate's airline pilot brother, Sam, flew down
from New York. Betty's brother and Jim's former roommate, Dave Howard, arrived from Costa Rica, where he
was serving with the Latin America Mission. The
memorial service was too soon for any other relatives to
come.

The rambling Saint house was crowded that evening,
with missionaries bringing in food and people huddled
in every room, talking, discussing the Aucas, recount-
ing treasured memories of the five martyrs. Around and
about slipped Capa, his camera clicking until he seemed
to fade into the woodwork.

"When I heard about the trouble," Dave Howard
said, "I went directly to Panama. General Harrison let
me into the Tunnel, where I followed the movement of
the rescue groups. While I was there, a call came to the
colonel who was plotting the progress. He listened a
minute, put down the phone, turned to us, and said,
'They just buried the last body.' I got here as soon as I
could."

Faces were turning toward Dave. The widows were
listening. "The military were very understanding and
expressed their sympathy when I told them Jim was my
brother-in-law. But they didn't really understand. Jim
Elliot was so much more. He was the closest friend I
ever had, my roommate, and best man at my wedding.
I loved him like a brother."

Dave was feeling this way, not wanting to sound
maudlin or overly sentimental, but trying to lift the
gloom.

"Oh, that boy was a rare bird. A scholar and a clown.
And Ed McCully, you got the two together and you had
a pair of comedians! I could tell you some stories. . . ."
And he did. They all did. And the remembering helped.

Tears were dried by laughter as they sat around Marj's kitchen and recalled days gone by.

"You didn't seem to think they were all that funny on your wedding night," Betty reminded her brother with a coy smile.

"Oh, well now, that was something else! See, Jim was best man at my wedding, and Ed was an usher at the Wheaton Bible Church. Afterwards four or five cars of friends, mostly 'forty-niners,' as we called our class, followed us into Chicago, to have dinner together. They had decorated our car with tin cans, paint, shoes, and stuff, and driving right behind us came McCully's red convertible, with the top down. We were all still in wedding regalia: white tux and bridal gown, and Ed had a straw hat. Well, they blew horns the whole way. Then, when we got into Chicago, at every stoplight they would blow and blow. People on the streets would look to see what all the racket was, and Ed would stand up on the seat, tip his straw hat to the crowd, and make a political speech! He told them he was running for mayor of Chicago—promised to put a refrigerator in every garage. Then the light would turn green, and off we would go. He'd do a repeat performance at the next stop.

"Well, all that was very funny, but, after dinner, Phyllis and I headed to the Sheraton Hotel for our wedding night. The bellboy led us upstairs to our room, but just before we turned the last corner, we heard this terrible commotion: a fight in the hallway! I knew at once that Elliot and McCully had found out our room number and were there ahead of us. Sure enough, they were putting on a performance in the hall. After persuading the bellboy not to call the police, they all piled into our room. About twenty of them in our wedding suite! Can you imagine?"

Dave looked around at the attentive faces. Expressions of sympathy and laughter had replaced the tense lines of tragedy that had been there for the past week. He felt the comic relief was just what they needed for a while, so he continued his tale.

"My first thought was, How can I get rid of this crowd? They stayed and stayed, joking and cutting up. I finally decided they'd never leave until I got Jim calmed down, since he was the ringleader. So I said, 'Jim, why don't you read a passage of Scripture for us?'

" 'That's a good idea,' he agreed, so I handed him my Bible, and he began reading from First Timothy: chapter one, chapter two—he just kept going. He read the whole six chapters! I didn't think he'd ever finish! Then, when he did, he turned to the crowd of kids sitting on the floor and said, 'What did you all get out of this?' No one said anything. 'Well, I'll tell you what I got out of it,' he said, and began a long Bible study, repeating the whole book!"

Dave's appreciative audience laughed understandingly. "I don't think he ever would have left if Betty hadn't dragged him out of there."

"I tried to point out to him how he would have felt if someone did that to him, but he just acted as if the thought hadn't entered his head," Betty said.

"I knew Nate fairly well at Wheaton, too," Dave told Marj, "but he was more mature than the rest of us. He was a bit older and had been in the service. He knew more where he was headed. I thought of him as a quiet, conservative, steady fellow."

"Oh, but he had a tremendous wit, too," Marj declared, with murmurs of agreement all around. "Nate wasn't the prankster, but he was quick with a turned phrase—could describe things so expressively. Like telling of an old plane in Mexico, he said that if the termites stopped holding hands, it would fall apart."

"That sounds just like Nate," one of the missionaries standing around said. "A few months back I heard him say, 'I'm not a preacher, just a pilot,' but then he got up in church and preached the best sermon I've ever heard."

"Yes," Marj agreed, "whatever he did, he did it wholeheartedly. If it was relaxing, tinkering, playing with the kids, or working, he gave it his best. Most of all, he had a real urgency to get the gospel out."

"Did you know Rog and Pete, too?" Marj asked Dave.

"I met Pete only once. He and Jim had dinner with Phyllis and myself one evening in Wheaton when I was in grad school. They were just about ready to go to Ecuador. Pete struck me as a delightful young man with a keen mind who also had a good sense of humor. He and Jim did a lot of bantering."

"Pete, I think, hung back a little more than Jim," Olive said, breaking in. "Ed was kind of in between those two, to provide a balance. Those three worked so well together. They were very close."

"I wish I could have known Pete better," Dave mused.

"I'm sorry you didn't know Rog," Barbara said with a smile. "I remember the very first time I saw him. It was at Northwestern Schools in Minneapolis, right after the war, when the soldiers were returning. I saw him walking down the hall in his paratrooper's uniform. So tall and handsome! He appealed to me from the very first moment I saw him."

"And obviously he noticed you, too."

"No," she replied wistfully. "Not really. We became

acquainted later in the missionary medicine class. We discovered we had common goals; that was the impetus of our relationship."

"Speaking of common goals, how long had the five fellows known each other?"

"Well, everyone knew Nate," Marilou answered. "And Jim and Ed and Pete were working together all along. They were the Brethren Boys, as Nate so often referred to them. Rog was the new one to the team, but he fit right in immediately. They all got along remarkably well. They had not only the common goal of reaching the Aucas, but they shared a total commitment to Christ. They really made a remarkable team."

Everyone agreed with that remark, but it also brought back the reality that in the morning they would be memorializing that remarkable team that had given its all.

The service was held in the chapel at the Gospel Missionary Union's Bible school. The school was on part of the land that Nate had obtained from the oil company.

The widows and the four oldest children were there: Barbara holding Beth; Marj grasping Kathy, with young Steve Saint on a bench behind; Marilou with her stomach swollen, trying to manage her active Steve; and Betty and Olive sitting nearby, with Olive holding her Bible tightly and staring straight ahead.

Capa clicked away during the first songs. Then a look of amazement came over his face and he moved to the side and quietly sat down. Later he explained, "I saw in the faces of those widows, at that one moment, a photographer's dream—the finest, most dramatic picture I could ever get. The expression, it was so beautiful; but I could not take the picture. It simply was not the time."

"There was a unity among us," Barbara remembered afterward. "Cornell says there was not a tear shed, but I don't think that's quite right, although we weren't sobbing and carrying on. We didn't go all to pieces. The whole time I felt, well, of course, everyone was praying for us. I sensed just a closeness with God: a calmness, a peace, and a knowing that God was carrying out His plan."

The next day when the bedraggled ground party arrived, Capa felt no restrictions about taking pictures. The haunted look in the eyes of Frank Drown and his companions who had buried their dear friends was captured on film. Capa then listened to the discussion in the Saints' kitchen, when the widows insisted they be told everything. They all felt it would be better to hear all the facts than to wonder for the rest of their lives. So they listened attentively as Dr. Johnston gently but candidly described the bodies and how they found and buried them.

While they sat listening, caressing the children, Capa glided around the room, using the camera's eye to capture the calm acceptance, the faith, and the peace that the widows portrayed in their time of agonizing loss. His pictures recorded the message of God's sufficiency more clearly than any words ever could.

Capa's six-page spread in *Life*, titled "Go Ye and Preach the Gospel: Five Do and Die," was reprinted by many news magazines abroad. The story, with Capa's vivid pictures, gave the waiting millions the raw details they wanted to know about the attempted contact with Stone Age savages, the sacrifice of five young husbands, and the unquenchable courage and faith of their young widows. The pictures of the widows holding their children were as touching as Nate's photos, recovered from Palm Beach, of their husbands and the three Aucas who had come in peace just two days before the massacre. Perhaps the most poignant picture of all was that of the hauntingly beautiful Olive, the bride left childless, grasping only her Bible.

The multitudes of Christians around the world who had prayed through the week of waiting now turned their prayers toward the widows. Capa wrote that each wanted to stay in Ecuador and serve the God their husbands had followed in obedience unto death.

There was much that *Life* and the media as a whole could not tell. What would the years ahead bring to the widows? How would the loss of their fathers affect the children? And what of the Aucas, for whom five precious, promising lives had been sacrificed in an attempt to tell them of One who had made an even greater sacrifice of love?

Before the widows separated (Betty and Olive to Shandia; Barbara to Macuma, the jungle station where she and Rog had worked; Marilou to Michigan for the imminent birth of her child; Marj to remain in Shell, at least until Nate's replacement arrived), they discussed the matter of the several people who wanted to be helpful by soliciting funds on their behalf. Dr. V. Raymond Edman, president of Wheaton College, was particularly zealous in this, and he joined with General Harrison and Clyde Taylor, executive director of the Evangelical Foreign Missions Association, as trustees of the fund for the widows and children of the five martyrs. This freed the women of the responsibility of receipting and distributing the funds.

Many people wrote to tell how the sacrifice of the five had touched them. Said one, "The story changed my life completely, making me realize how selfish and shallow I had become." A USAF pilot stationed in England wrote that he was applying to MAF. From Brazil, a missionary reported that a group of Indians had asked God to forgive their own apathy toward the spiritual needs of fellow Indians. In Quito, Protestant churches were jammed on the Sunday following confirmation that all were dead. Missionaries and national Christians wept openly. At Shandia, Quichua Christian backsliders renewed their vows to be faithful.

Robert Hill, pastor of a Freewill Baptist congregation in Richmond, Virginia, was one of thousands of United States pastors who preached about the sacrifice that Sunday. "There was a hush," he remembers, "and I could tell everybody was affected by it. It was the turning point for many members to become more involved in missions.

"One of the deacons came to me afterward in tears. 'I can hardly believe,' he said, 'that here are people dying to take the gospel and I will hardly walk across the street to talk to my neighbor about the Lord.' " The deacon, according to Pastor Hill, was never the same from that day on.

Responses to the stories in *Life* and *Time* were mixed.

"Let's use all our efforts to improve our own country and stay out of the jungles of Ecuador. I am sure it will cause the Auca Indians to give thanks to whatever god they believe in," wrote a *Time* reader from Villanova, Pennsylvania. In the same vein, an American Indian from Detroit criticized missionaries for trying to show tribal people "the right way. . . . Who is to say who is right and who is wrong?"

Others saw great potential good in the deaths on Palm Beach. A Nyack, New York, man reminded *Time*, "History shows that the death of martyrs does not stifle Christianity but promotes its advancement." A Philadelphia man assured *Life*, "By such means as the blood of martyred saints the seeds of the Gospel have been sown. Though tragic in itself and though little understood by the world, God's purpose is in it all."

Both secular and Christian newspapermen editorial-
ized on the incident. One of the most thoughtful articles
appeared in the *Portland Oregonian*.

If it hadn't been for the missionary zeal of the
apostles and their successors, Christianity would
not have become one of the world's great religions.

The five American missionaries . . . were carrying on a work begun by Peter and Paul nearly
two thousand years ago. Both Peter and Paul are
believed to have been brutally executed for their
efforts to convert Rome to Christianity. Thousands
of others in the centuries between have sacrificed
their lives in the same cause.

. . . Cartoonists have made a joke of missionaries sitting in giant stewing pots of cannibal chiefs,
but the risks and hardships of these devoted men
and women are no cause for laughter, as the fate of
the Auca expedition shows.

Why don't they stay home and let the benighted
heathen live as they like? Has not Christian missionary work accompanied or been followed by
economic exploitation of many races? Have not
vice and disease formerly unknown in isolated
areas followed in the footsteps of the preachers of
the Gospel? Are there not enough sinners near at
hand to be saved?

Questions such as these are asked by some who
cannot fully understand why men and women
should devote their lives to hardship, at bare subsistence pay, to spread their religion.

Unquestionably the effects of missionary work
have not all been to the glory of God. But without
the missionaries' zeal, Christianity quite probably
today would have been merely a small sect of an

older religion and would soon have ceased to exist. Few will argue that the world is not better for the spreading of the teachings of love and faith which are the basics of Christianity.

The forefathers of most of us were European savages or barbarians. Ufilas brought Christianity to the Goths, St. Patrick to the Irish, St. Columba to the Scots, St. Augustine to the English. Boniface brought the Gospel to Germany, Ansgar to the Scandinavians and Aladimir to the Slavs. Would Europe and America be as enlightened today if these men had not felt that strange force which still sends missionaries forth to preach the Gospel to every creature?

The missionaries to the Ecuadorian savages made their headquarters at an oil company camp. No one wonders why men invade the jungle to seek for oil.

Independent evangelical editors tended to touch this same theme. Denominational editors were more cautious, while praising the dedication of the five martyrs.

The one sour note came from the *Christian Century*, the organ of liberal Protestantism. Under the heading "Five Missionaries Die Needlessly," a *Century* editor, without any inside knowledge of what had happened, laid the deaths to "blundering" and "a thirst for publicity" by independent, fundamental Protestant missions. "Some of which," the *Century* said, were "legitimate but shallowly conceived Christian enterprises," while "others are hardly more than rackets whose main purpose is to shake loose the dollars of credulous and uninformed people." The denominational mission societies, the *Century* hastened to assure, "sought to conserve manpower" and insisted on "a high level of . . . histor-

ical, cultural, anthropological, and linguistic training"
for their missionaries. Ironically, in its next issue the
Century ran an article on humanitarian reasons for caring about Indians.

Readers blasted the *Century*. A Minnesota Presbyterian pastor called the editorial shameful. An Ohio
minister wondered if the *Century* was "willing to call the
martyrdom of St. Stephen a needless one." An Ohio
reader said, "By the same reasoning (as your editorial)
Jesus did not need to make that last trip to Jerusalem."

Beyond all the opinions expressed and commitments
vowed were the hundreds of letters from Christians of
like faith assuring the widows, "We'll be praying for
you and the children and for the Aucas, that soon they
may be reached."

"As the father of one of those boys, I'm here today to testify to you young people of the reality of God. God is real, God feels, God knows, God speaks, God sympathizes, God sustains and succors." T. E. McCully, father of Ed McCully, speaking at Wheaton College Chapel

The Families 3

"It's a boy!" Marilou McCully smiled at the expected news and the reassuring howl made by her healthy new son. It had been an easy delivery; still, she was thankful she had her sister, Billie, with her. Her family and Ed's had been sources of strength while she adjusted to the loss of her husband and the bearing of her third child.

"I think you should name him after his father," her mother-in-law said quite pointedly.

"No. His name is Matthew. Matthew Jay, for the Matthew of the Bible and his Uncle Jay. That's the name Ed picked out for him. He was so sure it would be another boy." She smiled again, remembering her tall, masculine husband. "He always said we would have five sons, and after that I could have anything I wanted."

Even before she was home from the hospital, reporters were asking for interviews and wanting Marilou to speak at various churches and rallies. She felt an obligation to talk about her experience with concerned Christians who had prayed for the fellows during the long week when their whereabouts were unknown, yet she

had a deep sense of responsibility to her young sons.
Stevie was four and Mike only one. With baby Matthew
only a few weeks old, she managed to speak to her
home church, First Baptist in Pontiac, Michigan, and a
number of other groups in the homeland.

"I believe that in spite of careful planning and all the
precautions they took, God allowed them to be killed,
because He knew they could be used in a greater way
through their deaths than through their lives," she told
them. "I am sure that only eternity will reveal the results."

While she was on speaking tours, her parents kept
the boys in Pontiac. Only Steve was old enough to express his longing for his father. "I know my daddy is
with Jesus, but I miss him, and I wish he would just
come down and play with me once in a while," he
pleaded. He displayed his brotherly love to baby Matthew one day when the baby was crying. "Never you
mind," he told him. "When we get to heaven, I'll show
you which one is our daddy." The tragedy was probably most upsetting to little Mike, who was still a baby,
too. Although he couldn't understand, Marilou felt he
must be confused by all the events that had changed his
life. She was concerned that there might be permanent
scars.

Besides the pressing responsibility of caring for her
boys, Marilou's greatest desire was to continue to serve
the Lord on the mission field. With three young sons, it
didn't seem practical to return to Arajuno on the very
edge of Auca territory. The perfect solution came when
she was asked to run a home for missionary children in
Quito.

Olive had stayed with Betty in Shandia for only a few
weeks following the memorial services at Shell Mera.
She could not speak Quichua and felt of little help. Pete

had not been at their jungle post of Puyupungu long enough to establish a strong base at which she might work. She thought it best to go home until something more definite opened on the mission field.

News that the wife of one of their martyrs was home spread quickly among the Plymouth Brethren. Speaking requests poured in from churches, youth organizations, and service clubs. "I was in Ecuador just over a year," she pleaded. But people wouldn't take no for an answer. They wanted to know everything about the Aucas, about the five men, and about the other widows. And when she spoke, they hung on every word.

Olive was barely twenty-four, married such a short time, and still not over the shock. The pressure was heavy. She always had to smile and be brave. She was asked the same questions over and over: "Why were your husband and the others killed? Why are the Aucas so savage? What are the wives doing? What are your plans for the future?"

At some places pastors gave an invitation for spiritual commitments after she spoke. Many young people came forward in tears, offering to take the place of those who died. Older women embraced her as if she were one of their daughters. Pastors and deacons praised her for having so much courage. "It's not me," she said truthfully. "I couldn't do it without the Lord. If He can use me in telling the story of the five fellows, I will be fulfilling at least part of the purpose for which they died."

While on the speaking trail, Olive had kept in touch with Marilou. Upon learning that Marilou was going back to take over the missionary children's home in Quito, she volunteered to accompany her and help with the three McCully boys.

After a time in Quito, Olive visited missionary friends at Shell Mera and some of the jungle stations. On January 8, 1957, just one year from the day of the Palm Beach massacre, she was in Shandia, with Betty. She pitched in and helped, then later wrote, "There has not been time to stop and think of the past, for the duties of the day filled our minds."

The duties of the day had kept Betty Elliot busy in Shandia. Besides caring for two-year-old Valerie, she taught in the Quichua school Jim had founded; helped with medical work; translated parts of the Bible into Quichua; and worked on a book for Harper & Brothers about the martyred men. She had never doubted her decision to return to Shandia after Jim's death. "I came to Ecuador to serve the Lord, not Jim," she said. "With him gone, my duty did not change."

Valerie was the ray of sunshine that lightened the sometimes too-busy days. She would follow her mother, barefooted, down slippery jungle paths, visiting sick Indians or just visiting, and was a joy to everyone as she demonstrated her father's charm.

At the end of a year without Jim, Betty reflected on her months alone in the jungle with Valerie and concluded, "Jesus Christ meant precisely what He said when He declared His grace to be *sufficient*. He is El Shaddai: the God who is enough."

Barbara Youderian was still living in the jungle with her children, Beth and Jerry. They had first lived a while in Macuma, where Frank and Marie Drown were stationed, then moved to Cangaimi with Dorothy Walker, a missionary nurse who became Barbara's partner.

Cangaimi was a small Atshuara village beside an airstrip that Roger and the Indians had hacked out of the virgin forest. He and Barbara had planned to move here after the Auca contact and carry on a school and medical clinic that had been promised to the Indians. Barbara and Dorothy were there to fulfill that promise.

Every two weeks the MAF plane brought mail, cargo, and critically needed foods. The pilot and a radio were the only contacts with the outside world.

They were two women and two small children alone among Indians who were just beginning to break away from a pattern of revenge killing and head shrinking. Barbara imagined that the Aucas looked and lived very much like the Atshuaras, who could have easily killed Roger while he was clearing out stumps for the airstrip.

Barbara felt no fear of these Indians, who sometimes appeared to listen raptly to Bible stories and sometimes acted as if they didn't care at all. She and Dorothy treated plenty of snakebite cases, yet they never saw a snake around the house where Beth and Jerry played. The Lord, Barbara felt, was watching over them.

Beth was past four now and still had clear memories of her daddy, with whom she had been very close. During language studies, she had been a familiar sight, perched on Rog's shoulders, tiny arms locked around his neck as he walked around practicing Spanish and talking to people. Later, in the jungle at Macuma, she often accompanied him to the barn and sat on a log while he milked and took care of the cattle.

Jerry had been only a baby when their father was killed. It was difficult to know how the experience might have affected him.

Barbara talked to them about their father when it seemed natural. Beth sometimes wished that her daddy would come down from heaven and ride her on his shoulders again. Their mother also told them about the Aucas. Almost every night, Beth prayed that the Indians who killed her father might come to know Jesus as their Savior.

Like the other widows, Barbara received stacks of mail. One request came from *Youth for Christ* magazine, asking for a short article for the first anniversary of Palm Beach on what the Lord had taught her during the past year. Barbara wrote:

> One year ago today the Lord met five young men fully consecrated to take the Gospel of Christ to those savage creatures of God, the Auca Indians. It pleased God to raise them from the beach and carry them home with Him safely to Heaven. I miss Roger very much; it is also very true that Bethy and Jerry need their Daddy's wise counsel and love.
>
> But not for one moment have I wished that Roger had not gone to Palm Beach for I believe today, more than a year ago, that it was the perfect will of God that he do so. . . .
>
> On seeing the little wrecked plane, my first thought was that perhaps one of them might be horribly suffering. Then a friend of mine reminded me of Phil. 1:29 ". . . to suffer for Him." Yes, there's a command to suffer, whether it be the fellows on the beach, we five wives, or perhaps one of you who are called upon to suffer for Christ in the homeland. We do not know what the Lord has for us, but whatever might come, we can say with Paul, "I can do all things through Christ who strengthened me."
>
> I believe the most important thing that the Lord has taught me this year is that of giving. Whether it be giving of myself, of my loved ones, or of my time, I cannot out-give the Lord, for when I give, He gives more. He has provided for me physically, spiritually, and materially.

As I look to the future, my thoughts are expressed in the following poem:

> I cannot, but God can;
> Oh, balm for all my care!
> The burden that I drop
> His hand will lift and bear,
> Though eagle pinions tire,
> I walk where once I ran,
> This is my strength, to know
> I cannot, but He can.

Marj Saint and her children had remained in Shell Mera for five months. She handled the radio, continued as hostess to visitors, and kept up with her three active children, doing much as she had done when Nate was alive.

When Hobey Lowrance came to replace Nate, Marj moved to Quito and took over the HCJB guest house so Kathy and Steve could attend the Christian and Missionary Alliance school just down the block. Here she played hostess to transient missionaries and guests visiting from outside the country.

During those months, a familiar sight at the HCJB house was Marj at the head of the table holding little Philip, with Steve and Kathy at her side. After dinner, when the kids were tucked in, she could be seen sitting by the fire, answering the letters that kept coming from around the world. She was determined to give a personal reply to everyone who had taken time to write and pray. Then, as her time permitted, she wrote the script for HCJB's radio program "Household of Faith."

In the year that had brought so much change to her life, Marj felt no bitterness. She, too, believed that God was all-loving in His sovereign purpose for Nate and his friends. She, like Marilou, Barbara, and Betty, also found inspiration and reminders of her loved one in his children. In Kathy's clear blue eyes with their built-in twinkle, she could see Nate. Watching Steve talk or hearing his voice made her visualize his father. In little Philip she saw Nate's smile and dimple. The children were more precious than ever.

There were times when Marj found it hard to believe that Nate was gone. Often, in her memory, she was at the radio, hearing Nate call, "Preparing to land at Shell Mera, over and out." Then she would call Kathy and Steve and they would run out into the yard and have a contest to see who could first see the yellow speck in the sky. "Now," Marj wrote for the *Youth for Christ* anniversary article, "instead of watching for our daddy to come in the air we have a new anticipation for the fulfillment of 1 Thessalonians 4:17, 'Then we which are alive and remain shall be caught up together with them in the clouds, to meet the Lord in the air: and so shall we ever be with the Lord.' "

Most of all, the five widows expressed gratitude for the peace and assurance the Lord had given them in their lonely days. Despite the sorrow and the vacant places, it had been a year of spiritual triumph. They could rejoice as a group, when they were all together in Quito for Olive's visit (the first time since the memorial service that they were all in one place), that they had found richer fellowship with God. His promises had not failed.

Public interest in the widows continued high. The Saint house in Shell Mera became a popular place with Christian tourists who wanted to see the radio nook where Marj had talked and the table around which the widows sat when they heard the final report. Articles and news notes about the widows keep appearing, including a second spread in *Life*, by Cornell Capa, about the widows, "who are gallantly carrying on in Ecuador the work for which their husbands died."

One fact that seemed to escape many of the visitors and writers was that the five martyrs were not only husbands and fathers but also sons, sons-in-law, brothers, and friends. Many lives besides the widows' were personally touched by grief at their death.

When the men were discovered to be missing, their parents had to be notified in the United States. Pete Fleming and Jim Elliot had agreed that, in case of mishap, Jim's folks were to be notified first, and they would tell the Flemings. The senior Elliots had spent several weeks with Jim and Betty at Shandia and were aware of the dangers of harm from jungle Indians. Pete had told his parents very little, knowing they had wanted him to stay home and teach at a Christian college or seminary. Their other son was in Africa, and they felt one should remain in the homeland.

Unfortunately, just the reverse of what the men had planned happened. Pete's folks received the telegram first and were stunned. An hour later, reporters were on their doorstep, inquiring about Pete and Operation Auca. "We didn't even know he was going in there," they sobbed. "We can only pray that he will come out alive."

Pete's brother, Kenneth, was in a Zulu village far back in the South African bush. A friend happened to mention seeing a newspaper story about five missionaries being killed in Ecuador. Thinking that Pete might be involved, Ken tried to get the paper but couldn't. Days later, a cable from his folks reached him.

Fred and Clara Elliot heard from the Flemings. The Elliots' oldest son, Bob, lived near them in Portland; their second son, Bert, was home on furlough from his missionary post in Peru. Their daughter, Jane, was a receptionist at Wheaton College, where her new husband, Dr. Gerald Hawthorne, taught Greek. She heard over HCJB that her brother was missing. "We sat by the radio every night," she remembers, "praying that Jim might be alive. Then, on Thursday we heard the worst. It was such a terrible shock. Nothing like that had ever happened to our family."

Family had always been very important to the Elliots. From infancy, the children were taken to weekly services and prayer meetings at the Plymouth Brethren assembly. The parents read the Bible daily in the home and the entire family went camping with fellow believers from other Brethren chapels.

Among the Plymouth Brethren there is no hierarchy. Every believer is considered a minister for Christ, although certain functions are reserved for men. Fred Elliot often traveled as a preacher among Brethren chapels; sometimes he was gone for weeks. Clara held the family together, and the children prayed for their father while he was conducting meetings. An elderly English woman lived with them, helping with the children, so that Clara could continue her chiropractic practice that helped support the family financially. Her office was in her home, for she wanted to be near in case of an emergency. "My family comes first" was always her motto.

Between college and his service in Ecuador, Jim had spent a year with his parents while speaking at various chapels and schools in the area. Between times he would work with his father at his construction jobs. While putting nails in paneling for a Brethren assembly hall or wrestling with a plumber's wrench, Fred would instruct his son in the deeper meanings of faith. Jim was humbled to discover that in experiences of putting God first in his life, Fred had discovered many of the theological concepts his son had been taught at Wheaton. Jim had always been close to his mother; but that year was a special time of growing for the bond between himself and his "Beloved Dad," as he addressed his father in intimate letters that described spiritual adventures that could only be shared with a kindred spirit.

The last time all six Elliots had been together was in January 1949, for Bert's wedding, but there were no regrets at Jim's going to Ecuador. The family considered itself privileged to have two representatives on the foreign field. "I surely praise God for the valiant way you both took my going," Jim wrote from the ship after his parents had seen him off at the Portland docks. "I know very little about how you feel at seeing me leave. All I understand is that it must be very keen, and closely linked with all that this life involves for you."

Fred and Clara yearned to visit their sons in South America. Finally, they sold a piece of property and took Jane with them to Peru. After spending several weeks with Bert, they flew to Ecuador to be with Jim and Betty for the birth of their child. Together, father and son made several missionary journeys among the Quichuas, with Fred preaching and Jim interpreting. Fred put his building knowledge to use in helping repair missionary houses. Then Betty's time came, and Valerie was born in Shell Mera at the Saints' house. The senior Elliots were a bit disappointed that Jim's first child was not a son, but one look at the beautiful little granddaughter ended that.

They spent their last week in Quito with Jim, prowling through the old Spanish city that is so steeped in colonial tradition. They saw Jim for the last time at the Quito airport as they left for home. Jim stood straight and tall next to Betty, who held their newborn: Jim with his auburn hair gleaming in the sparkling high-altitude sunlight; Jim with his red Pendleton jacket flapping in the breeze.

Now Jim was dead. Fred wept unashamedly and profusely. "Why couldn't God have taken me instead?" he asked Clara, who was sobbing also. "He was so young. He had a whole lifetime of service to give the Savior. Why did he have to die?" He and Clara clung to each other, and their tears mingled in the heartbreak they felt over losing their son.

"Well, we know God's on His sovereign throne," Fred said at last. "God allowed him to be killed, and there must be a purpose. Maybe we can't see it. Maybe we'll never see it, this side of eternity. Yes, there has to be a purpose. He wouldn't have taken him otherwise." For consolation, they turned to each other and the Scriptures upon which they had built their home. And the peace and acceptance came. They couldn't understand, but they could trust.

Another strong couple who lost a son was Lawrence and Katherine Saint. In one way they were of a different mold from the other parents. Nate's father was a notable artist who made some of the stained-glass windows for the National Cathedral in Washington. Five-year-old Nate had been the model for the boy with the five loaves and two fishes in one of the panels. Nate's mother was a Wellesley graduate who had specialized in the history of stained glass. In another way they were like the Elliots, for they were strict fundamentalists. Their seven sons (Nate was next to the youngest) and daughter all bore biblical names. Movies, card playing, alcohol, tobacco, and comics on Sunday were taboo for the children. Radio listening was regulated. Yet they were fun-loving. Lawrence built a double-track roller coaster in the backyard. The family frolicked on picnics. The boys hunted and fished. But when doors of the nearby Baptist church were open, all the Saints went marching in.

Sam, who became a commercial airline pilot, was the oldest. Ben, who became a pastor, was the baby. Rachel, the only girl, was interested in missions. Nine years older than Nate, she regaled him with missionary stories about Robert Moffat and David Livingstone, cannibals and crocodiles.

The family all knew that Nate's flying over jungles was a dangerous business, but he was doing it for the Lord, so they trusted Him to keep Nate safe. When they received a letter written just before Christmas 1955 in which Marj added a postscript prayer request for "the matter of extreme importance which we can't name yet," they prayed, but they didn't understand just how perilous the project was. When news came that Nate was missing, they were shaken. But they all believed that whatever the outcome, God would watch over Nate.

When the report came that Nate's body had been identified, brother Phil, an artist-evangelist, was in language school in Costa Rica, preparing for missionary service in Argentina. He wrote an article paying tribute to Nate and their parents. To understand a man like Nate, he said, "you must visualize a mother and dad who taught their children out of the old family Bible, who faithfully took their children to the little country church, who prayed over them, and at times wept over them, but who never gave up the fight to keep them from the power of the evil one and lead them into the will of God."

The family was concerned about the impact the news might have on Katherine Saint, but she, too, bore up bravely. She was encouraged by a statement from Marj: "God took the dearest treasure I had on this earth, but the future looks as bright as the promises of God."

For Roger Youderian's parents, acceptance of their loss was perhaps the hardest of all. Armenian descendants of Christian immigrants who had fled from genocidal Turkish Muslims, they were professing Christians but not very active in their church.

The Youderians were quiet, law-abiding farmers, with seven children. Roger, the baby of the family, was always the one who put the interest of others before his own wishes. He had enlisted in the army, thinking this might keep his married brothers from being drafted. He later dropped out of Bible school for a while to work and help support four nieces and nephews. Then, after graduation, he took time out to help his sister pay medical bills.

When news came that Roger was missing, they thought of all the dangers he had faced as a paratrooper in World War II. He had even survived the bloody Battle of the Bulge. Surely death would not overtake him on a lonely strip of beach in the verdant Amazonian jungles!

When the unthinkable was confirmed, his family was understandably grief-stricken. They bore their burden bravely, and whatever reservations they might have had about their son's going to the mission field were not divulged to the newspapers.

The McCullys in Milwaukee were the most prominent of the parents. January 9 was their daughter Peg's birthday, and they took her and her husband out to dinner to celebrate. Returning home from this happy occasion, they were informed by the babysitter that an emergency call had come from Marilou's mother in Michigan. After learning that Ed was missing in dangerous territory, they phoned Ed's brother, Jay, who was at the Marquette University Medical School in Milwaukee. As was customary in their family, they prayed.

The McCullys had spent seven weeks with Ed and Marilou the year before and vaguely knew about the Aucas, but they thought their son and daughter-in-law were busy with the Quichua work. They hadn't considered them in any danger and were jolted by the news.

Precious scenes concerning the boy of whom they had been so proud filtered through their memories: Ed slipping softly into his father's study at age seven to ask, "Dad, can you tell me how to be saved?"; Ed, growing up to be the ideal boy—handsome, athletic, personable, a leader; elected to head his Wheaton class; winning the national oratorical championship; admitted to law school, with great expectations. Then he announced: "Dad, Mom, I've been battling with the Lord for weeks. Last night I surrendered my life completely to Him. I won't be going back to law school."

Just three weeks before the fatal day, T. E. McCully had resigned his executive position in the baking industry to become the executive director of the Christian Businessmen's Committee International. A popular speaker in Christian circles, he declared, "I want to give God all the years I have left." His position put him in the public eye, so it was natural that the press would turn to him for quotations when it was known the five men were dead.

"If you had known Ed would be killed this way, would you have still wanted him to be a missionary?" one callous reporter wondered.

"Yes," the elder McCully responded quickly. "God demands our all, and He has a right to it."

Over and over he was asked why the young men had gone on such a dangerous venture. "It was their love for Christ and their willingness to go anywhere He might lead. Jesus said, 'Except a corn of wheat fall into the ground and die, it abideth alone: but if it die, it bringeth forth much fruit' (John 12:24, KJV). Ed's mother and I believe that the blood of these five young missionaries will be the seed of the Auca church.''

T.E. spoke at the memorial services for Ed that were held in Milwaukee, then to a Youth for Christ rally in Chicago, where the big man drew applause and an out-pouring of vows to take Ed's place from young people. As his statements were reported in the press, invitations to speak came from colleges, churches, and business groups in over a dozen states. He accepted almost every one, flying, sometimes driving—any way he could get there—saying, ''Anything, Lord, anything You want, I'll do.''

T.E. was an inspiration to thousands. In her own quiet way, so was his wife, Lois, who went with him on many trips. She had devoted her life to her husband and three children. During the days of adjusting to Ed's death, the deep roots of her faith, planted by her own godly parents, held. The sense of loss would never leave, but neither would the firm conviction that God in His wisdom had a higher purpose for her son's life.

The story that had the attention of the nation and many other western countries for a week did not die. After the first-line reports came the magazine articles, the first-anniversary stories, and follow-up reports. Palm Beach and the men who were killed there, along with the challenge of the Aucas, would remain before the public for years.

The five martyrs were the most-lauded missionary heroes of their generation. Their sacrifice and the bravery of their wives were also inspirations to thousands upon thousands of nonchurch-goers. The letters and phone calls to the families kept coming.

In an unprecedented way, the martyrdom of the Palm

Beach Five stirred students and faculty at evangelical colleges. The slain missionaries were memorialized; at Wheaton, Nate's, Ed's, Jim's, and Betty's alma matter; at Northwestern College in Minneapolis, from which Roger and Barbara had graduated; at Moody Bible Institute, which had more missionary alumni than any other school in the world and proudly counted Marilou among them; at the Bible Institute of Los Angeles, at which Ed and Marilou had taken a course in missionary medicine; and at many other Christian institutions as well. Hundreds upon hundreds of youth stood in college chapels and cried their willingness to take the gospel to the ends of the earth. Old-timers said there had been nothing like it since the pulsating rallies of the Missionary Volunteer Movement in the first decade of the twentieth century.

Olive came back to the States over a year after the killings and found the interest still high. She couldn't possibly speak to all the groups requesting her appearance. Marj, on furlough with her family in Idaho, then visiting friends in California and Nate's family in Philadelphia, showed slides from Nate's film recovered on the beach. She gave a ringing challenge for missionary service that moved many. She journeyed to New Zealand and discovered the Auca story was as well-known there as in the United States. She spoke to the International Youth for Christ Congress in Venezuela and saw many young people coming forward to make Christ Lord.

The continuing phenomenon puzzled some clerics and theologians in denominations unaccustomed to missionary fervor. They could not understand why so many could get so stirred up by the death of five young fundamentalists trying to reach a little tribe of Indians in the backwaters of a small South American country.

Other denominational churchmen, more missionary minded, simply felt too many personnel were being allotted to reaching small groups like the Aucas.

Hollywood came calling. The producer of the successful inspirational movie "A Man Called Peter" and the agent for the popular television series "Playhouse 90" both wanted to produce a dramatic film on the five martyrs and their families. The widows said no to both offers, fearing commercial filmmakers might take too many liberties with the facts.

The women did gladly cooperate with Abe Van Der Puy, who wrote an updated account that was condensed in the August 1956 *Reader's Digest*. And they did agree that Betty should write a book for all of them about the experience. The book, *Through Gates of Splendor*, was released by Harper & Brothers about the same time as the *Reader's Digest* story hit newsstands and mailboxes. Within two months it was outselling two other Harper books that were on the *New York Times's* best-seller list. However, *Through Gates of Splendor* did not make the *Times's* ranking, because religious bookstores are not polled in determining best-sellers.

While the widows turned their backs on Hollywood, they approved a Christian film by the same title as the book. They further agreed that all earnings from the book and the film should go to the Auca Missionary Foundation, established by T. E. McCully, Sam Saint, and Betty Elliot's father, Philip Howard. The receipts were designated not just for the Aucas, with whom missionaries were not yet working, but also for the cause of spreading the gospel throughout the world.

This fund had nothing to do with the Widows' and Children's Fund set up by Dr. Edman. That fund now held around $75,000, which was to be held in trust for the children's education.

Dr. Edman also played a key role as press agent. "Prexy," as he was called by Wheaton students and alumni, was known as a quiet and gentle man. His role in promoting the Auca story revealed that he could be an aggressive promoter of the causes for which he seemed most concerned, Wheaton College and the reaching of the Aucas. At one time, Edman had been a missionary in Ecuador and dreamed of taking the gospel to the Aucas himself.

"There is no need for faith where there is no consciousness of an element of risk. . . . In our going into Auca territory there were risks aplenty."
Elisabeth Elliot
The Savage, My Kinsman

The Entry 4

T he spotlight had been on the five martyrs and the widows. There was hardly a word in the press, secular or evangelical, about the work of Rachel Saint, who, for almost a year before the five attempted their contact, had been working with Dayuma on the hacienda.

This lack of attention was due, at least to some extent, to the fact that the other missions had certain misgivings and reservations about the program in which the Wycliffe people were involved.

Some missionaries objected to Wycliffe planes serving Catholic priests and nuns in isolated locations. Others didn't approve of the philosophy of utilizing two organizations: the Summer Institute of Linguistics and the Wycliffe Bible Translators. Home-country supporters usually regarded Rachel and her co-workers as "Wycliffe missionaries." But in Ecuador they served under SIL, a legally separate sister organization that had an official working agreement with the Ecuadorian government.

Besides Wycliffe, there were three other evangelical missions at work in the area: the Plymouth Brethren, the Gospel Missionary Union, and the Christian and

Missionary Alliance. The World Radio Missionary Fellowship (HCJB), like MAF, served the entire evangelical community as well as providing essential public services to the country.

Although each was independent, the missions cooperated in matters of mutual interest. The Alliance, for example, sponsored a Christian school in Quito for children of missionaries. The other organizations, including Wycliffe, each provided a quota of teachers.

The Alliance, the GMU, and the Brethren also informally divided the eastern jungle territory among themselves so as to avoid any appearance of competition. The Alliance took the northern part, the Brethren the middle, and the GMU the south. The divisions were not set in concrete and there were frequent crossovers in cooperative ministry, but in general each group worked its own territory. It happened that the Auca area lay in Brethren territory; for this reason, the Brethren Boys saw the Aucas as their responsibility. Nate and Roger were only assisting them.

Wycliffe, guided by the vision of founder "Uncle Cam" Townsend, was promoting Bible translation for every Bibleless group in the world. Following his blueprint, Wycliffe's sister organization, SIL, contracted with governments and universities in many lands to do linguistic work among the language minorities.

The SIL contract, signed with the Ecuadorian government in 1953, provided that SIL would work among linguistic minorities with unwritten languages, produce alphabets, compile grammars and dictionaries, and translate books of high moral value. Translation of the Christian Scriptures was not spelled out in the agreement; it was understood that this could be included under books of high moral value.

Shortly after the agreement was signed, Uncle Cam

presented the Wycliffe "pioneers" for Ecuador to President Velasco Ibarra. When he introduced Rachel as a future worker among the Aucas, the sprightly-little-bald-headed man's eyebrows flew up. "Aucas, did you say? Once I flew over an Auca village and they threw spears at the plane. No outsider has ever lived in Auca territory. What makes you think you will?"

"God will make a way," Rachel replied.

The president shook his shiny head doubtfully.

Rachel had been waiting for that opportunity since 1949, when on her way to Peru she stopped off to see Nate and Marj. Nate had told her about the tribe whose territory he avoided flying over. "They've never taken kindly to outsiders," he said. "No one has ever been able to live with them."

This was the first time Rachel had heard about the Aucas. "My heart was strangely drawn to them," she wrote. *"If there was ever an unreached tribe, I thought, this was surely it."*

Rachel went on to Peru, for Wycliffe was not then working in Ecuador, and filled in for furloughing translators among the Piro and Shapra Indians. While with the Shapras, she became acquainted with the notorious headhunter Chief Tariri who had welcomed Doris Cox and Lorrie Anderson into his domain. "If two men had come, I would have killed them both and taken their heads," he told Rachel. "If a man and a woman had come, I would have speared him and taken her as a wife. But two women came calling me 'brother.' What could I do but protect them?"

The translator Rachel had been substituting for among the Shapras returned from furlough. Back at the Wycliffe center in Yarinacocha, Peru, in the group dining room, Rachel was having a meal with two friends, Catherine Peeke and Mary Sargent, and Uncle Cam, who at that time was living there. Catherine and Mary had been trying to locate monolingual Zaparo Indians on the Pastaza River near the Ecuadorian border. They asked if Rachel would be returning to the Shapras. "No," Rachel said, "I'm going to the Aucas."

"But they're in Ecuador."

"I know, but I believe God will lead me there."

At that moment, Uncle Cam stood up to read a letter from the Ecuadorian ambassador to the United States, inviting SIL to come to Ecuador.

So Rachel went to Ecuador with the determination to live among the Aucas. Since she could not live there yet, the next-best strategy was to find a speaker of the unwritten language who had come out of the tribe. It happened that Catherine and Mary had been unable to locate enough Zaparos in Peru, so they went to Ecuador also. Catherine joined Rachel in asking around Quito about Aucas who had left the tribe. "See Don Carlos Sevilla," a government official recommended. "He is a frontier rancher with a hacienda in the jungle and knows more about Aucas than anyone. We call him the Daniel Boone of Ecuador."

They found Sevilla to be a charming raconteur who loved to tell about his daredevil tangles with Aucas. He claimed to have fought them in hand-to-hand combat; once he fled eight days through the forest while burning with fever from a maggot-infested spear wound. He didn't believe any outsiders could ever live among the fierce Aucas and plainly intimated that the two American señoritas were of less than normal intelligence if they decided to try. When Rachel insisted that she intended to learn the Auca language, he shook his head, turned both hands palms up, shrugged, and said, "I have four Auca girls working on Hacienda Ila. You are welcome to stay at my house and talk with them."

Rachel immediately accepted his invitation and Catherine accompanied her, continuing her Zaparo language studies. But upon arriving in February 1955, they were disappointed to find that only one of the four had not forgotten the Auca language. This one, a young woman named Dayuma, had fled the tribe in her early teens and was now around twenty-three or twenty-four. She had borne two children, only to lose her Quichua husband and one child in a measles epidemic. The surviving child, a boy of five, clung to her skirts and stared at the strange visitors in wide-eyed wonder.

"Will you help us learn your language?" Rachel asked.

"*Si, si.*" Dayuma nodded assuringly. But the next morning she went to the fields at sunup and did not return until after sundown. With a young son to care for, she had little time left in the evening.

Catherine continued to search for speakers of the little known Zaparo language in Ecuador. Rachel stayed at the hacienda, doggedly snatching every possible minute to talk with Dayuma. From their catch-as-catch-can conversations and from a small word list prepared by a German anthropologist over a quarter century before, Rachel began building an Auca vocabulary and a rough grammar.

As Rachel began to understand Dayuma, she realized that most of the Auca woman's memories were of spearings and revenge murders. Her fears seemed to focus on an Auca killer named Moipa. "He speared my playmate Gomoki's father," she whispered to Rachel one night. "I watched him die. Then he speared her mother and little sister and tried to drown Gomoki and another girl."

Another evening Dayuma recalled a clash involving all her close relatives. When the spears stopped flying, her father, Tyaento, dragged twenty-two bodies into a mass grave. From then on Dayuma became tortured by the fear that her father might be killed and, by Auca custom, she would be buried alive with him.

Dayuma told Rachel of the time her father had returned empty-handed from hunting. "The monkeys I hit refused to die. I am cursed," he said. A few days later one of her relatives ran into the clearing, shouting that Moipa had killed her grandfather and wounded her father. Dayuma ran, shrieking, into the forest.

Hours later she came upon another escapee, who reported that Moipa had come to the clearing and attacked women and children. "He hacked one of your sisters to death," the informer said. "He may have killed your mother, also."

Dayuma had to know. She sneaked back and found her mother, Akawo, alive. "Go with me to the outside," the girl begged. "We will all die here."

Akawo refused. "The outsiders are cannibals. They will only kill and eat us."

Dayuma would not be deterred. She and her cousin Umi never stopped running until they came upon a camp of Quichuas. The Quichuas took the naked girls to the hacienda, where Don Carlos gave them clothes and a place to sleep.

Rachel also discovered that Dayuma was haunted by a fear of spirits. She talked about jaguars that had lived inside her grandfather's body. "They would ask grandfather, 'Who are you angry with? Tell us and we will kill them.'"

Another night she mentioned to Rachel, "There is a devil in the forest who attacks at night, sucking the blood of the Aucas until they are dead. That's what grandfather said."

Did the Aucas believe in God? "Yes, grandfather told

us that in the beginning God created three men and three women. When the women grew big, the men cut open their stomachs and the babies popped out. The women died, but the children survived."

The Aucas also believed in life after death. "When you die, your body rots in the ground," Dayuma said. "Your soul rises high in the sky to a small trail. There you will meet a worm as big as a tree trunk. If you jump over the worm, you can go farther up in the sky. If you are afraid and turn back, you will turn into a termite."

Would those in the sky live forever? "No, grandfather said they will die. That is what grandfather said. That is what I believe." Rachel gleaned such frightening tales of Auca lore from months of patient questioning of Dayuma.

Sometimes she and the Auca woman could only communicate by sign language, acting out words. Rachel would repeat an expression over and over until Dayuma approved of the pronunciation. Then Rachel spelled it phonetically so it could be written down. The abundance of such Auca words as *kill, spear, die, blood, bodies,* and *grave* was appalling.

The work moved at a snail's pace. Often, because of Dayuma's work regimen, there were days when Rachel had no time at all with her. By late 1955, when Jim Elliot came calling, the Wycliffe linguist was still working on the basic structure of the language.

Jim gave not the slightest hint of the secret project in which he was involved. Rachel was not even told that Nate was making flights over Auca territory. Consequently, she didn't think it unusual a few weeks later when she was asked to stay in Shandia with Betty Elliot while Jim was away.

Rachel only learned of Operation Auca when Marj called Betty to report the damaged plane on Palm

Beach. With the worried wives, Rachel waited for word of the missing men. When news came that they were all dead, she shared their grief, but her overwhelming sympathy was for the widows. Rachel had "only" lost a very special brother. Since she was nine years older than Nate and his only sister, she had helped mother him from his earliest infancy. When he was just a little boy, still called Thany, she had told him stories of heroes and conquerors, missionaries and martyrs. And now he was a martyr, too, and she felt she had lost both a brother and a son.

Added to the hurt was the knowledge that he had been in on an attempt to reach the Aucas and had not told her. He had known of her interest in and concern for the tribe for years. She had spent nearly a year trying to learn the language so that she might go to the tribe and give them God's Word; for the past weeks, Nate had been planning and working toward an attempted entry and had kept it a secret from her.

Rachel recalled Jim Elliot's visit and his desire to learn a few Auca phrases. Now the purpose was clear to her. She couldn't understand why Jim hadn't just explained, but that didn't matter. That didn't hurt. But Nate—Nate hadn't confided in her.

Then Marj handed her a letter. As she took the envelope marked "To be held until further notice," she realized he had thought of her after all.

"Dear Sis," she read with tears welling in her eyes, "Last night, Jim, Ed, Johnny, and I reached a hard decision." Certain phrases leaped from the page. "Reaching the Aucas had been on our hearts for a long time. . . . Hard not to share with you the efforts. . . . We trust God to carry us forward . . . that Christ might be known among them. Affectionately, Nate."

The sacrifice of Nate and his friends—her friends,

too—and now the letter made her doubly determined to learn the language. One day, she was sure, Christ would be known among the Aucas.

Then a special letter came from Uncle Cam.

> I was in Sulphur Springs [Arkansas] when word came that the five young men were dead. I knew that one was your brother, and I knew of your high regard for one another. The news drove me to my knees, and while I was praying, I heard myself saying, "Lord grant that one day Rachel will be able to introduce the man who killed her brother to the president of Ecuador, as her brother in Christ." I shall persevere in that prayer until the day God grants it.

The worldwide press coverage brought a motley crew of journalists, anthropologists, and soldiers of fortune to Ecuador. The most persistent came to Hacienda Ila to photograph and interview the Auca women. Some of the braver, or more foolhardy, asked Dayuma to guide them into Auca territory. "No," she said to each one, "I will not go until God tells me."

Meanwhile, Rachel received copies of pictures developed from Nate's film recovered on Palm Beach. She showed Dayuma photos of the friendly Auca visitors, George, Delilah, and the older woman.

"Aunt Mintaka!" Dayuma exclaimed excitedly. She thought the girl was her baby sister, Gimari, but couldn't be sure. Nor could she positively identify the man. But she was certain about the older woman and talked animatedly about her and other relatives.

Rachel again told Dayuma the story of Palm Beach and why the five men had risked their lives. Over and over, Dayuma said she was sorry her people had killed Rachel's brother and the other "good foreigners."

Dayuma was extremely curious about Rachel's belief that she would meet her brother again. How could a dead body come to life? Rachel painstakingly explained the story of Lazarus to her, then asked Dayuma to repeat it. When Dayuma came to the place where Jesus commanded, "Lazarus, come forth," her eyes shone. This encouraged Rachel and her new temporary partner, Mary Sargent, to think that Dayuma might be a true believer. But they couldn't be sure yet.

After Hobey Lowrance, Nate's replacement, flew into Shell Mera with a new plane in June 1956, MAF and Brethren missionaries in the area resumed the spiral drops to the Aucas. Flying low over an Auca clearing near the massacre beach, MAF's Johnny Keenan and a MAF colleague, Grady Parrott, spied three young Aucas, one dressed in a shirt dropped by the slain missionaries. They dropped a pair of swimming trunks and a shirt and received friendly waves in return. This revived hopes that at least the younger Aucas might be ready for friendship with the outside world. They felt it would be good to fly Dayuma over the village and allow her to speak to her people through the loudspeaker. Rachel objected. "It's premature. We don't even know if Dayuma is a true believer—or what she might say to her people. Moreover, the mission would be dangerous, and if anything happened to her, we would lose the only reliable Auca language helper there is. We must be patient and go slowly."

The men respected Rachel's decision and continued the gift drops. Encouraged by the response, Dr. Wilfred Tidmarsh, who had first invited Jim Elliot to come to Ecuador, built a hut in Auca territory that was six hours walk from Arajuno. Tidmarsh, whose doctorate was in geology, had been praying to reach the Aucas for years. Since the martyrdom of his younger colleagues, he had become more venturesome.

Tidmarsh hoisted a model of the MAF plane to the top of a wooden post and kept a lantern burning on the ground all night. He stayed alone in the hut during the week and returned to Arajuno only on weekends.

On Monday morning he came across Auca footprints near the house. Later he came back from a weekend in Arajuno and found the house a shambles. The vandals had left two crossed spears in the open doorway and had pushed a spear through each window. Pages from Jim Elliot's Bible were on one of the spearheads. This didn't strike Tidmarsh as particularly friendly.

Meanwhile, Uncle Cam Townsend had been busy in the States. He, like Dr. Edman, thought the world must be kept informed about the continuing Auca story, especially about the roles of Rachel Saint and Dayuma, of whom so little was known. Some Christians in the homeland mistakenly thought Rachel was Nate's widow.

Uncle Cam wanted the evangelical public to see the Aucas as an example of the millions still without any Scripture in their language. He believed publicity about Rachel, Dayuma, and the Aucas could help create a ground swell among Christians for "finishing the job" of translating Scripture into the estimated two thousand Bibleless languages. He also wanted to get Dayuma to the United States, where she could give Rachel full-time help with the language.

He was quite aware of other tribes that rivaled the Aucas in bloodletting and revenge killing. Some had recently been entered by Wycliffe workers, but none of them had killed any missionaries. None had ever been given such publicity in *Life*, *Time*, and other big organs of the media.

Uncle Cam did not see this as exploitation, as some

would charge later. To him it was a matter of striking while the iron was hot and the attention of the Christian world was focused on the Aucas.

The Wycliffe leader did not have the aversion to Hollywood that some evangelicals had. Through friends, he planted the idea with Hollywood's Ralph Edwards that Rachel should be honored on the popular TV show "This Is Your Life." The way was opened to get Dayuma to the States, where Uncle Cam knew she would be warmly received.

He called on Don Carlos Sevilla, Dayuma's patron, told him about the honor to be conferred on Rachel, and asked him to keep it a secret from her. Would the "Daniel Boone of Ecuador" go to Hollywood and appear on the program with Rachel? How could Don Carlos resist such an invitation? Could Dayuma accompany Rachel? The hacienda owner instantly agreed she could.

"One more thing," Uncle Cam pressed. "If Dayuma is to appear on television, Rachel will have to interpret. Could you arrange to let her off work a little early in the day so Rachel can improve her understanding of Auca?" Don Carlos immediately said yes to that, and the problem that for two years had hindered Rachel's work was solved.

Rachel thought Carlos Sevilla was the one to be honored. When they got to Hollywood, she was told they were going to rehearse a TV interview. She was talking with Ralph Edwards on a platform decorated with palms and a thatched hut when her father walked from backstage. Then her brother Sam Saint and some old friends came. Finally, Chief Tariri, now a Christian, walked in before the cameras, wearing his most impressive headdress and beetle-wing earrings. The show was live and was seen by an estimated 30 million viewers.

After the show, Dayuma came down with a high fever. Dr. Ralph Byron, Jr., a noted Christian physician, was called to the hotel. Dr. Byron, with Rachel interpreting, told Dayuma of his faith in Christ and asked if she was a believer, too. "Yes," she replied in Auca. "I think of Jesus day and night." Fortunately, the fever passed quickly.

With Carlos Sevilla's permission, Uncle Cam arranged a trip across the country for Dayuma. They stopped at the University of Oklahoma, where young missionaries-to-be were taking the Wycliffe language course. From there they went to New York, where Rachel and Dayuma were the featured attractions of the Billy Graham Crusade in Madison Square Garden. After hearing Dayuma's testimony of faith, hundreds came forward to make decisions for Christ.

After stopping off at the Saint home in Pennsylvania, Rachel took Dayuma to Wycliffe's biennial conference in tiny Sulphur Springs, Arkansas. Again, Uncle Cam was there to present Rachel and her Auca language helper to hundreds of Bible translators. Dayuma, in turn, learned about tribes she had never dreamed existed.

On November 18, 1957, electrifying news came from Ecuador. Two Auca women had come into a Quichua outpost, and Betty Elliot had gone there to meet them. Rachel wanted to return to Ecuador immediately, but Dayuma was afraid. "Tell your friends to take the visitors and get safely away. My people will come and kill." A few days later, her fears were confirmed when Aucas attacked, killing the Quichua who had first received the two women and taking his wife captive.

Betty took the two Auca women to Shandia, where they would be safe and she could begin Auca language study with them. Taped messages flew back and forth between Shandia and Sulphur Springs. Dayuma recognized the women as her aunt Mintaka, who had been on Palm Beach, and Maengamo, Uncle Gikita's wife. The women told Dayuma her mother and little sister were still living, but many other relatives had been speared to death since her departure.

In one taped message, Mintaka mentioned that Moipa, the Auca killer Dayuma feared most, was dead. Dayuma gave a whoop of joy, but when Rachel pressed her about going back to her people, she was still fearful. They continued language study, with Rachel making more progress in a month than she had made in a year on the hacienda.

Rachel spent much of the time narrating Bible stories, then having Dayuma give them back. When they came to the baptism of the Ethiopian eunuch, Dayuma repeated in Auca the Ethiopian's request, "What does hinder me to be baptized?" and Philip's reply, "If you believe with all your heart, you may."

They went on to other material, but two weeks later, Dayuma suddenly asked, "What good man of God can enter me into the water?" Rachel immediately thought of Dr. Edman and his long interest in the Aucas. He had spent the previous Christmas in the jungle, had been flown over Palm Beach, and had written many articles and news reports on the Auca challenge.

Edman had a son living near Sulphur Springs, so Rachel wrote Wheaton's Prexy a note, inquiring if he would be coming any time soon to visit his son. If so, would he baptize Dayuma? Edman was so excited at the proposal that he asked Christian industrialist R. G. LeTourneau to fly Dayuma and Rachel to Wheaton for the baptism. He felt the baptism of the first Auca convert should be something special. "It would be most appropriate," he wrote Rachel, "to have the baptism in Wheaton, from which three of the five martyrs went on their way toward the gates of splendor."

The ceremony was set for April 15, 1958, in the Wheaton Evangelical Free Church, then pastored by Wilbur Nelson, a former pastor of Marj Saint's. Fred and Clara Elliot came from California to visit their daughter Jane and to witness the historic event. Mrs. T. E. McCully and a number of evangelical mission leaders were honored guests. Dayuma dedicated her eight-year-old son, Sammy, to the Lord, then Edman immersed her before the congregation. It was for this, Prexy declared, that the five men had given their lives.

The Wheaton College news office dispatched press releases. The Chicago newspapers ran stories that were picked up across the country. For good or ill, the baptism of the first Christian Auca was another media event.

From Chicago, Rachel, Dayuma, and Sammy flew to New York, where they were the guests of Sam Saint and Cornell Capa in the fashionable Gold Room at Idlewild Airport. Harper wanted Rachel to write Dayuma's biography. Betty Elliot had only recently finished *Shadow of the Almighty*, the biography of Jim Elliot, based largely on Jim's journal; if a third book could be produced, Harper would have the beginning of a series of jungle missionary stories. They were confident a new book would be another best-seller, but Rachel said she could not spare the time.

As they flew south toward Ecuador, Dayuma grew anxious about the reunion with her two relatives. "I will call you Nimu. That was the name of my little sister Nimu, who was hacked to death by Moipa," she told Rachel. "That will make you my sister and their relative." She warned Rachel not to inquire about details of the Palm Beach killings or the women might think she was planning to avenge her brother's death.

The emotional meeting took place at Wycliffe's new jungle base, Limoncocha, where palm thatch huts had been built for the Auca women. Dayuma, Mintaka, and Maengamo talked for days about what had happened in the tribe during Dayuma's absence. Rachel and Betty hung close by, trying to understand what they were saying, and several times they heard Dayuma telling Bible stories.

M and M, as the missionaries called the two Auca women, accepted Rachel as *Nimu*, meaning "star," and Dayuma accepted Betty as *Gikari*, meaning "woodpecker," the name M and M had given her. When the buds of the kapok tree, which produces a cottonlike substance used by the Aucas for wadding around darts to fill the bores of blowguns, began to swell, the Auca women said, "We promised to return when the kapok is ripe. You must come with us, Dayuma. Your mother waits for you."

Dayuma wanted very much to see her mother and her younger sister, but she was afraid to return to the tribe. "There will be trouble if you don't come with us," M and M countered. Reluctantly, Dayuma agreed to go with them if Rachel would care for little Sammy. "If all goes well," she said, "I will return for him, with an invitation from relatives for you and Gikari to live in the tribe."

Rachel and Betty told the three women good-bye, not knowing if they would ever see them again. Rachel wrote a letter for Dayuma to Dr. Edman and other prayer supporters on September 2, 1958, the day they left, telling of their departure and asking for special prayer. Edman circulated the letter to Wheaton's mailing list, and it was printed in hundreds of church bulletins and Christian publications. Thousands of Christians were praying that Dayuma and her relatives might open the door for missionaries to live in the long-resistant tribe.

Rachel took Sammy and went to help translator Bobbie Borman in the Cofan tribe while Bobbie's husband, Bub, was away on a survey. Bub had been in the ground search party that had buried Nate, Jim, Pete and Roger.

Betty returned to Arajuno, where she had been staying with the Tidmarshes, and continued making overflights into Auca territory with the MAF pilots. She made two trips and searched for a glimpse of Dayuma, Mintaka, or Maengamo. When she could not spot any of them, she felt great concern for their safety.

Cornell Capa came for another visit. As on previous trips, he and Betty talked about the value of photography. Capa convinced her that a photograph could often tell a story much better than words. "Simply let your camera be the extension of your eyes," he told her. "Then take lots and lots of pictures."

During their long conversation, she confided to Capa that her only motive for wanting to reach the Aucas was her love for these people for whom Christ had died. "The fact that Jim loved and died for them," she added, "intensifies my love."

"But what about taking little Val into a tribe of killers?" he questioned.

"Where I go, she goes. I trust the Lord to take care of us and the results."

Marj Saint, who had been keeping up with the exciting recent developments, flew in with two of her children, Philip and Kathy. They would keep Betty and little Val company at Arajuno while the Tidmarshes went into Quito. As Marj stepped out of the plane, she exclaimed to Betty, "Wouldn't it be wonderful to see three Auca women coming down the airstrip?"

On Thursday morning, September 25, Betty was spreading clothes on the grass to dry in the sun when three Quichuas arrived from the Curaray River. After the usual exchange of greetings, Betty asked if they had heard any news of the Auca women. One of the Quichuas casually remarked, "They came out." Trying to contain her excitement, Betty prodded them for more information and learned that seven Auca women and three Auca boys had left the tribe and were on their way to Arajuno.

At Betty's shout, Marj came running. They started walking down the airstrip, with Valerie between them. "Jesus loves me, this I know," came a voice singing in English. Betty recognized Dayuma and raised her camera. Dayuma, Mintaka, Maengamo, and their companions emerged from the tall grass.

After the warm, joyous welcome, Dayuma assured Betty that she and Rachel would be well-received by the tribe. "They know you are good foreigners and will not kill you."

"But your people speared my husband," Betty said. "Will they spear us, too?"

"No, Gikari," Mintaka assured her. "They will not spear a woman. You will be like our mother. They will honor you and Nimu. It is the downriver people who spear."

Betty sent word to Rachel, inviting her to join the group. As quickly as possible, Rachel made the trip. There was no question but that she would go with Betty and Valerie to live with Dayuma's relatives. They packed a radio and provisions for a long stay. Along with her Bible, Betty packed notebooks, camera, and film. Heavier items were set aside to be airlifted later.

On October 6, 1958, Rachel, Betty, and Valerie left Arajuno with the ten Aucas and five Quichua men who served as carriers. On foot and by canoe, sleeping in leaf shelters at night, in two days they reached the Tiwaeno River, a tributary of the Curaray, and began working their way up the smaller river. Poling their canoes around the bend, they came face to face with a bronzed, naked man and two women, standing like sentinels in front of a cluster of a half dozen little huts and two large roofs supported by long poles. They were Kimo and his wife, Dawa, and Dayuma's younger sister, Gimari, the "Delilah" of Palm Beach.

"Where are the others?" Dayuma asked.

"They went downriver for a new supply of food," Kimo explained. "I remained here to welcome the foreigners we hoped would come."

Rachel and Betty were overjoyed. At last they were living among Aucas in Auca territory. It had been thirty-three months to the day since the massacre on Palm Beach. While the adults began unpacking, Valerie, who would soon be three, sat on a log, eyeing Kimo.

"Mother," she asked finally, "who is that man? He looks like a daddy. Is he *my* daddy?"

Betty smiled and said, "No," and continued with her work.

Night fell and they all gathered around a fire. The Quichua carriers, who would be staying overnight, began singing hymns. Then Fermin, the one who had carried Valerie into the tribe, voiced a prayer of thanks for "bringing us safely to these new friends. Show us how to live together like brothers."

*"The foreigners are with us here. We are
learning about God and want to live well."*
Uncle Gikita, one of the Aucas who killed
the five missionaries

Rachel and Betty 5

   owering forest trees on the west and south and
   the clear-running Tiwaeno River on the north and
east surrounded the clearing in which Rachel, Betty,
and Valerie made their new home among the Aucas.
Rachel hung her hammock in the hut occupied by Dayuma's uncle Gikita and his wife Maengamo and their
children. Betty moved into a smaller, adjoining abode,
where she could lay Val's blanket sleeping bag on a
platform of split bamboo.

Rachel had lived with the Shapras and Piros in Perú,
and Betty had spent nearly a year with the colorful Col·
orados of western Ecuador before marrying Jim and
moving among the jungle Quichuas. With this background, the women knew the wisest course was to
make themselves at home among the people and to
blend in as quickly as possible.

The adjustment was easiest for little Valerie. Running
about the small clearing, her blond head and white
body contrasting with her dark-skinned playmates, she
felt no fear. She had her mommy and her doll, a yard
without a fence and with logs and stumps to climb on,
and cool water nearby to splash in. She was quite con-
tent in this little world.

It wasn't quite that simple for the women. They knew
the risks involved in their undertaking, but they chose

to exercise their faith by going ahead with what they were assured was God's will for their lives. Still, it was impossible to wipe out thoughts of others who had followed similar leadings and had met the same cruel fate their loved ones had at Palm Beach. These Indians made no hostile gestures and seemed, in fact, to be quite friendly. Yet Arthur and Ethel Tylee had lived among the Nhambiquara Indians in southwestern Brazil for nearly two years before the Indians unaccountably turned on them and slaughtered Arthur and their infant daughter, leaving Ethel critically wounded.

Such thoughts were brushed aside as the women busily "scratched on paper," as the Aucas explained it. The Indians thought this a curious occupation, but it was deeply serious to the women, who were determined to learn the language as well and as quickly as possible. Without the right words, they could not express the message they had come to give.

Although a good deal of their time each day was spent simply living in the jungle, Rachel's and Betty's main priority remained language study. They wanted to identify with the people as much as possible as far as eating and living conditions were concerned; but, even while going about such lowly tasks, their ears were always attuned to new words.

The Indians showed remarkable patience with the two foreign women, often pronouncing a single word dozens of times, saying, "Do you hear, Gikari? Do you hear, Nimu?" When patience wore thin, one might say in disgust, "You are without ears." The building of their vocabulary list was no simple task, for so-called primitive languages are actually exceedingly complex.

They discovered that many word roots had six or more suffixes and had to be filed under a number of topics. The language was also rich in sound effects, especially in hunting and fighting narratives. One man came back from hunting and told of hitting a wild pig with a spear. He used one word for describing the sound of the spear as it hit the pig, another for the sound of the pig when the spear hit him, and a third for the sound the pig's body made as it hit the ground.

Some words exploded out of the lungs. Others were produced with a sucking in of the breath. There were some sounds that were difficult to describe.

One of the most frustrating difficulties was that their good and faithful companion, Dayuma, had been out of the tribe for so long that she had forgotten some of her own language. After years of speaking Quichua on the hacienda, trying to learn Spanish, and picking up some English while in the States, Dayuma's grasp of her own language had understandably slipped. Being back in the tribe soon rectified this; she remained their best language helper and often helped clarify meanings and correct mistakes. The linguists were careful, however, not to use her as their only source of information.

Betty and Rachel shared their linguistic findings but kept separate files. Although Betty was not a member of Wycliffe, she had studied linguistics in the SIL program at Norman, Oklahoma, which was available to any qualified person needing basic instruction in how to learn a language that had not been written down. Because they were using the same techniques, the women were able to work together on the language. They also held to the same fundamental doctrines of the Christian faith yet were members of different denominations and mission organizations and were not officially a team.

Besides their differences in affiliations and an age gap of thirteen years, the Wycliffe woman and the young Brethren mother had had very different environments during their formative years.

Betty grew up under highly educated, strongly disciplined, and authoritative parents. The Howard house in suburban Philadelphia was kept immaculate; proper English was to be spoken; meals were served on time; and rules were not negotiable by the children. Everything was exact. Her editor father, from a literary family, spoke distinctly, used good syntax, and kept a dictionary near the dining-room table to settle any arguments that might come up about the meaning or pronunciation of words.

Her siblings and playmates were boys. Self-conscious of her tallness, she chose her words carefully and spoke directly and often bluntly. Jim Elliot had once told her, "You come across like a sledgehammer."

Whatever Betty did, she did to the best of her ability. Her father had taught her to be keenly observant. He would remember the color of a visitor's socks and the shape of a dinner guest's thumbs. His influence was revealed in the descriptions of the Aucas and their lifestyle included in the book Betty later wrote for Harper's.

Rachel also grew up in a household populated with brothers, but her parents, Lawrence and Katherine Saint, were from another Philadelphia suburb and were artists by training and temperament. Exactness and godliness were never equated. Meals were eaten at odd hours, and a large pot was kept warm on the stove so that anyone could eat whenever he wished. Self-expression was encouraged. There was no thought of punishing a child simply for failing to make a bed or being late for school.

In her mother's absence, Rachel was often in charge of her younger brothers. She learned to cook, clean, and keep her charges from turning the house into pandemonium. She entered the Philadelphia College of the Bible as an independent and strong-willed individual.

Before coming to the Aucas, both women had learned to live independently. Rachel had worked with alcoholics before joining Wycliffe and while in Peru and Ecuador had never been assigned a permanent partner. Betty had spent a year in mission work before marrying Jim and as a Brethren missionary was more independent than members of some other missions.

If they had had psychological evaluations before going to the tribe, probably no group would ever have tried to put the two highly motivated, independent personalities together. Yet their do-or-die spirits, their willingness to risk all for what they were convinced was obedience to God's will, had brought them together in the most isolated, primitive, volatile tribe then known in South America. Their common commitment to Christ and to bringing His message to the Aucas had brought about their alliance.

The worldwide publicity that had focused on the tribe since the killing of the five missionaries less than three years before did not make their task any easier. There had been little successful work among isolated tribes, so Betty and Rachel had to pioneer, living each day as it came, facing problems as they arose, and following what seemed to them was best for the Aucas. Their personal Christian commitment and their example before the world and their adoptive people demanded that they cooperate. It didn't mean they always had to agree or even approve of each other's point of view.

By Dayuma's best estimate, there had been about two hundred of her relatives in the group when she was a young girl. Trying to get a census and to determine how many were left was no easy task. Some had huts farther back from the Tiwaeno River, at intervals of a half mile or so apart, and came and went from the larger clearing.

Betty and Rachel started with a list of names and relationships of those in the immediate clearing and added
others as they came to visit. The final tally was fifty-six,
including sixteen Aucas from a downriver branch who
had fled upriver for the same reasons Dayuma had
escaped to the outside. This left only forty of Dayuma's
approximately two hundred kin alive. Four-fifths of her
people had died, most from spearings since her childhood.

The toll of revenge killings could further be seen in
the way the present population was balanced. The fifty-
six included only seven husbands. Uncle Gikita had two
spouses; Dabu, the brother of Gikita's wife Maengamo,
had three. The other five husbands were monagamous.
The rest were widows and children, some belonging to
families, some fatherless, some complete orphans. Two
of the widows, Dayuma's sister Gimari and Ipa, had
been married to Naenkiwi, the "George" of Palm
Beach. They said he had been speared and seriously
wounded about a year after the five missionaries were
killed. He was buried alive, according to Auca custom.
Little Bai, his baby by Gimari, was to have been thrown
into the grave with him, but Gimari grabbed the child
and ran; now he was alive and toddling around the
clearing.

Betty and Rachel frequently heard talk of the downriver clan of more-distant relatives. They were "bad
people" who "lived by spearing," Uncle Gikita said.
Beyond these bad people, Dayuma's family knew of
only one other Auca couple who lived far away, near
the Napo River.

There had been no need to speculate on which of the
men living in the clearing had participated in the Palm
Beach killings. Mintaka and Maengamo had identified
the five killers to Dayuma, who had passed their names

on to Betty and Rachel. Gikita had been the leader. The others were Kimo, one of Maengamo's brothers; Dyuwi, who was married to Dayuma's sister Oba; Nimonga, a more-distant relative of Dayuma; and Minkayi, Dayuma's half-brother.

M and M had given the missionaries a sketchy idea of what had happened at Palm Beach. It seemed that the Aucas had wanted the men to take them to Dayuma in their "wood beetle" (the plane). When the five did not respond, Naenkiwi ("George") declared that the men had come to kill and eat them. He had persuaded the warriors to attack. Betty and Rachel wanted more details, but it was obvious that none of the killers wanted to talk about it. Perhaps they were ashamed. Perhaps they didn't feel it was proper to talk about the spearing of men who were relatives of the two women now living among them. Whatever the reason, the two foreign women agreed with Dayuma that it was best to wait patiently and not press for more information.

There appeared to be no chief or council of elders with authority within the group. The older women seemed to get the most respect, yet their commands were not always obeyed. The only social unit seemed to be the family. The husbands appeared to be only slightly in command, with wives frequently disobeying or disregarding requests. Each night Dabu would choose from among his three spouses which wife he would eat with and which would share his hammock, and these were not necessarily the same.

The Aucas seemed utterly uninhibited about nakedness or bodily functions. Clothes were only a novelty. Except for the kapok-fiber strings around the wrists, waists, and thighs, they wore only large balsa-wood plugs in their earlobes. They wore their coarse, black hair cut in bangs from ear to ear, with their hair in back dropping below their shoulders.

They appeared to be amazingly healthy, yet their essentials for living were few. A hut could be built in a day or two. Hammocks took longer to weave but lasted for years. They also had clay pots, fishnets, baskets, drinking gourds, blowguns and poison-tipped darts for killing small game, and spears for hunting large animals and for warfare. They lived solely from nature's bounty and did no buying or selling. The only Auca creature comforts were hammock and fire.

Men hunted and fought the battles. Women tended the gardens, but both sexes gathered fruits and nuts from the wild. Men, women, and children joined in fishing with spear, net, or bare hands. Mornings and evenings each woman cooked, then tossed the food on plantain leaves for her family to eat without utensils, ceremony, or conversation.

In the evenings, everyone relaxed in their hammocks, stretched beside ever burning fires, and talked animatedly about events of the past or of that day. Any occurrence could provoke vigorous conversation and laughter. Once an aluminum pot of Betty's fell to the ground. "Did you see that? Gikari's pot fell!" From hut to hut, the announcement spread around the clearing.

It took Betty and Rachel a while to sort out what children were born of what parents. A child's father's brother was also called his father, as his mother's sister was called his mother, and cousins were called brothers and sisters. They soon realized that everyone in the group was close kin to everyone else.

Betty tried to evaluate the good and bad traits within the tribe. She noticed "no vanity or personal pride, no covetousness, avarice, or stinginess." Each man brought game home for his wife, or wives, but game was also shared with families who had little that evening.

Men did not beat their wives. Children were only lightly disciplined, and sometimes they received no correction at all. Drunkenness was unknown, for they did not make a fermented drink.

Still, there was a cruelty that deflated any illusions of innocence. Unwanted babies and infants born with abnormalities were strangled or simply left in the forest and allowed to die. When a father was killed, his dependent children were buried alive with him. The spearing of any enemy, down to the last low moan, was described with relish.

Children teased and sometimes tormented pet monkeys. Another sport was dropping hot coals on live toads. The favorite recreation was spear practice on banana trees, with the men showing their sons how to kill enemies.

Whenever Betty or Rachel mentioned visiting the downriver people, Dayuma's relatives said, "No, they will kill us."

"Well, don't you kill people, too?" Betty retorted.

"No, no, Gikari," Dabu insisted. "We just kill the downriver ones."

Betty compared the sins of civilized people—murders, abortions and child abuse, assaults, rapes, thefts—with the sins of the Aucas. She considered that they had killed her husband and his four friends in the belief that they were defending themselves. Didn't "civilized" people kill with even greater savagery in perceived self-defense? She felt forced to ask herself: "What do we mean when we speak of one people as being more 'needy' than another? What do we mean by 'savage'?" She was faced with the fact that socially she had nothing whatever to offer the Aucas. Man, whether civilized or so-called savage, had only one overwhelming need: Christ's redemption from sin and self. She concluded that the only reason she had for living with these people who had killed her husband was to obey Christ and give witness to His love.

Rachel could agree that the Auca's greatest need was Christ, but she felt Betty was too naive about the noble savage. Before their entry, Rachel had worked with Dayuma for almost three years and lived with her for months at a time. She kept remembering the horror stories from Dayuma's past: the spearing of her father and grandmother and so many others. The scars on the bodies of those in the clearing bore ample evidence that they were a violent people.

The Aucas, Rachel had come to believe, were not just another isolated tribe but a people who killed when they felt frustrated or enraged. Rachel noted in her journal that Dayuma's mother had seen the spear-killing of her father, two sisters, a brother, her husband, a son, a daughter, a son-in-law, plus many other relatives.

The tensions of tribal living began to show after a few months, and they decided it was time for a rest. Rachel and Dayuma went to Limoncocha, where young Sammy had been left in school. From there they flew to Quito, where Dayuma taped a selection of Bible stories in Auca. A representative of Gospel Recordings took the tape to Los Angeles for reproduction on four small phonograph records (for easy playing in the tribe).

Betty was welcomed in Quito by Marilou McCully, who was busy mothering the children at the missionary home next to HCJB. Marilou had reserved a special room with a fireplace for Betty, so the cool, damp air in the 9,000-foot-high-city would not seem too drastic a change from the jungle. The two enjoyed catching each other up on news of friends and family.

Barbara Youderian and her two children were still out among the Atshuaras. Marj Saint stayed busy as hostess at the HCJB guest house just down the block and was helping writer Russ Hit produce a biography of Nate that would be called *Jungle Pilot*.

Olive had returned to the States again, this time to stay. She was working as a secretary to the president of Shelton College in New Jersey when she met the president of the school's alumni association at a winter homecoming celebration. "I've been wanting to meet you," Walter Liefeld said, "to tell you how much your serenity and confidence in God has meant to me and many other people."

"We've become very good friends since," Olive wrote to the other widows in Quito. "He's a young Brethren preacher who is working on his doctorate in New York City. A wonderful Christian." The widows read between the lines of her letter and hoped she had found a new partner for life.

Early in February 1959, Rachel and Dayuma returned to Auca territory. Betty and Valerie waited until the end of March and brought Marilou McCully with them. Marilou was excited at the prospect of meeting the people for whom she had prayed so long. On the trips in and out, they were escorted by Christian Quichuas who had overcome their deep-seated fear of Aucas.

Rachel and Betty introduced Marilou around the clearing. Kimo gave her a broad smile. "He's one of the five Aucas who speared the fellows," Rachel informed her in a nonchalant tone of voice.

"Oh?" Marilou replied, her eyebrows up. "He seems like a sweet, peace-loving Indian who wouldn't harm anybody. It's hard to imagine him as a killer. Does he have any idea of what he did? Does he know how deeply we were hurt?"

"We can't tell," Rachel said with a sigh.

Marilou was a little appalled at the food Betty and

Rachel ate—mostly the same diet as the Indians: monkey meat, bananas, and manioc. They did have some instant coffee, tea, and powdered milk for Val. She was also struck by the lack of possessions. Betty had two cereal bowls, two cups, and a container for mixing Val's milk. She owned very little else, not even a mirror. The only "luxury" item was Rachel's typewriter.

After her arduous trip back to the nearest Quichua settlement, Marilou was approached by an Indian whose son had been killed by the Aucas. The woman stood silently for a moment, varied emotions playing on her face. Finally the Quichua asked, "Does your mother-in-law still cry because her son died?"

"Yes," Marilou told her compassionately, for she knew how very much Lois McCully still hurt.

Tears swelled in the eyes of the Quichua woman. "I do, too," she said softly.

Betty and Rachel found their lives falling into a pattern. They would spend three or four months in the tribe, devoting themselves to intensive language study; then one or both would take a short rest outside. They didn't always come and go at the same time, for they didn't really function as partners, just two women with a common goal.

In Quito, Betty and Val always stayed with Marilou, and Rachel and Dayuma stayed at the Wycliffe guest house. Rachel and Dayuma were collaborating with Wycliffe writer Ethel Wallis on *The Dayuma Story* for Harper. Uncle Cam had repeatedly tried to get Rachel to write the book, but she insisted she did not have time. Not one to take no for an answer, he had arranged for Miss Wallis to take the assignment. He was determined to use every means to keep the public aware of the Bibleless tribes and the need for dedicated young people to do linguistic work among them.

Harper was extremely pleased with the books on jungle missions. *Through Gates of Splendor* had sold over a hundred thousand copies in hardcover. *Shadow of the Almighty*, Betty's biography of Jim, was not far behind. Russ Hitt's *Jungle Pilot*, the biography of Nate Saint, was doing well. *Two Thousand Tongues to Go*, the story of Wycliffe, was also in the bookstores, as was *Mission to the Headhunters*, the story of Frank and Marie Drown's work among the headhunting Jivaros. *The Dayuma Story* was in production, and Betty Elliot's third title, *The Savage, My Kinsman*, would later be ready for publication.

This gave Harper seven titles in the series that marked the beginning of a new era in evangelical book publishing. Five of the seven were directly related to the Auca mission. Most had resulted from Cornell Capa's trips to Ecuador and his contacts with jungle missionaries. Capa provided many of the photos and served as picture editor for all seven books, besides preparing four major picture-and-text articles for *Life*. However, he did not make the bonanza some thought, for he contributed much of his time and work to the missionaries who prepared the books.

Betty took Valerie to the United States to visit Val's grandparents. Here she completed *The Savage, My Kinsman*. When the book was released, many evangelicals were shocked at her defense of the Auca lifestyle and her photos of naked Aucas. A few Christian bookstores considered some of the photos indiscreet and refused to stock it.

Because of the books she had written, Betty had established herself as an author. Harper was eager for her to write more, but she still believed her calling was among the Aucas.

*"For us to be willing to live with them cut
straight across the pattern for revenge. . . .
One day they found that our men had had guns
with them when they were attacked and that
they could have defended their lives. But they
chose to die rather than shoot the Indians.
Nothing less than this kind of commitment
would have broken the Aucas' cultural
mindset."*
Rachel Saint

The Truth Discovered 6

After almost two years with the Aucas, Betty and Rachel had devised the prototype of an alphabet, could speak the language haltingly, understood some of the grammatical system, and were beginning a rough translation of the gospel of Mark.

Dayuma, still the only believer, had been the teacher, preacher, and evangelist all along. She had made clothing for nearly everyone. When the first group picture was taken, it was Dayuma who arranged the people so that those with clothing stood in front, covering the naked bodies but not the smiles of the ones standing in the back row. Dayuma also taught her people to count days in units of seven and conducted a worship service in Kimo's and Dawa's house at sunup on the first day of the week, as well as giving informal Bible talks in the evening around the fires.

The Aucas had creation stories in their folklore. They lived in fear of evil spirits and curses and recognized certain people as having evil powers. The bad downriver Aucas, they said, had many witch doctors, but there was only one, the widow Tyaenyae, among the upriver clan. Whenever someone became sick, they blamed Tyaenyae for casting an evil spell and threatened to spear the old woman if the person died. Except for the consciousness of a creator and devils, their lifestyle was void of religion. They made no incantations or prayers to any deity.

Not surprisingly, Dayuma patterned her Sunday services after what she remembered from worship with missionaries and American Christians. "I'm going to speak to God," she would announce to the informal congregation that lounged in hammocks and sat on logs, squinting against the morning sun that was rising above the trees. "Stop talking. Close your eyes as if you're going to sleep."

Her morning prayers would run on and on, naming every missionary she knew in Shell Mera, Limoncocha, and Quito and every person she could recall meeting in the United States, including Dr. Edman and Billy Graham. She asked God to protect her people from devils, jaguars, snakes, and enemy spears. She besought Him to help the Aucas believe in Jesus and follow "God's Carving" so they would live well and stop spearing. When a member of the congregation interrupted, as often happened, she would say, "Shut up," then go on with her petition.

She led them in one-line hymns, chanted over and over in the familiar, nasal, singsong minor key used in singing about hunts and spear fights. She strung Bible stories together on a theme, embellishing as she went along, supplying understandable illustrations from daily life, keeping a sharp eye on her audience to make sure that everyone was paying attention. She concluded with a call to love God, believe in His Son, and live well.

Sunday after Sunday she kept this up, drawing from her repertoire of Bible verses and stories, going to Rachel and Betty for more Bible knowledge, then passing on what she learned to her relatives. Her congregation varied in size. One Sunday she might have only a dozen and another time thirty, for the Aucas were always coming and going from hunting, fishing, working in their gardens, and visiting among the scattered families in the area.

The nightly Bible talks were more informal, when members of the clan gathered around their fires for warmth in the jungle dampness. Dayuma did most of the talking, but frequently Gikari and Nimu entered in, with Dayuma adding their interpretations to be sure everyone understood.

Old Gikita would sit back in the shadows, watching; big, balsa earplugs framed his weathered face as he turned over new thoughts in his mind. His father had taught him about witchcraft and demons, but this new teaching from "God's Carving," as Dayuma called the Bible, was utterly new. Kimo would lean against a log, taking in every word, sometimes laughing at miracle stories from the Bible. The idea of a man walking on water! How absurd! Behind him young Dyuwi would frown, his face a ridge of resentment. Dyuwi still didn't trust the foreign women Dayuma had brought back with her. His fear of foreigners dated to his childhood, when he had been shot by one.

Kimo's wife, Dawa, often hung around after the others retired to their hammocks. She was weary of hatred and bloodshed. Every time Kimo started sharpening his spears, her fears heightened. "I want to believe in Jesus and live well," she told Dayuma. "But Kimo does not like your teaching, and he still hates all foreigners."

"Believing, you shall have your sins taken away," Dayuma assured her.

Dawa's interest kept growing. Rachel thought she was already a believer. The hard lines around Kimo's mouth relaxed, and he seemed to be more open. But until Easter 1960, no one was willing to profess faith before the group.

On this Sunday morning Dayuma called the people together as usual to hear a message from "God's Carving." She told the story of Jesus from birth to ascension winding up with God's judgment on those who rejected Him.

"All who do not believe will be thrown out, just as you throw worms out of your corn. Do you understand? That's how it will be. Not believing, the devil will take you.

"Who will say, 'Yes, I love God. Yes, I believe. Yes, I want to live well and take God's trail to heaven?'

"Will you, Dawa?"

"Yes."

"And you, Gimari, will you?"

"Yes, I will love God. All of us will love God."

Dayuma named others, but no one else would voice a commitment.

In September 1960, Betty and Valerie went to Quito for a visit. Rachel and Dayuma took Kimo and Dawa to Limoncocha. The young Auca couple saw where wood beetles lived (the hanger), watched a tractor pull out tree stumps, rode on a motor scooter, and, at sunset, learned to play volleyball with the "good" foreigners. They went home with plenty to tell.

The foreigners were back in the tribe until January; then they made another trip out. When they returned on February 19, Kimo met them with a smile. "We counted the days, and on God's day we spoke God's

Carving," he said. Could he be a believer?

A couple of days later, they heard Kimo announce to the group, "Now I will talk about Jesus." For a half hour he lay in his hammock, repeating Bible stories he had heard from Dayuma. When he finished, young Dyuwi prayed out loud for the first time.

Dayuma's Sunday message was on forgiveness. "See that monkey out there, tied with the vine? Well, that's the way we are tied to our sin, until God sets us free and cuts the vine. See the water in the little river? Believing in Jesus, our sins will be buried in water deeper than that." She closed with the story of Chief Tariri's conversion. Dayuma had previously told the group that Nimu had lived in Tariri's tribe for a short time before coming to Ecuador. "Now that he believes," Dayuma said, "the Shapra chief has stopped killing and shrinking heads. Now he teaches his people about God."

Later that morning, the Indians gathered around the radio as Rachel talked to Limoncocha. After finishing her regular sked, she picked up an Indian voice from Peru.

"Tariri!" Rachel whispered.

"Tariri!" Dayuma repeated. "He's the one I was telling you about. What is he saying, Nimu?"

Rachel translated as much as she could and guessed at the rest. "He's saying, 'Since I believed in Jesus, I live well. Instead of killing, I try to love and help everyone, even my enemies.' "

A few days after this, Dawa casually mentioned, "Uncle Gikita is now like Tariri. Talking to God, he goes to the forest."

The next significant sign of a spiritual movement came as Dayuma was finishing a Sunday morning lesson. "When the foreigners assemble, they ask those who know for sure that God has cleaned their hearts to say so. Who will speak what God has done in his heart?"

Dawa said immediately, "I did not live well before. Now I love God with all my heart."

Dyuwi, the youngest of the five Palm Beach killers, began counting on his fingers. "I killed this one and this one," he enumerated. "That was before I knew Jesus. Now He has cleaned my heart."

Kimo, another of the killers, counted his victims, then declared, "Jesus' blood has washed my heart clean. Loving Him, I live."

No one else said anything. That afternoon, Nimonga, another of the killers, came over to Rachel. He sat quietly on a log, holding his little daughter.

"Nimonga, did you understand what Dayuma spoke this morning about forgiveness of sin?" she asked.

"Yes."

"Will you say no to God?"

"No, I will not."

Rachel then had a long talk with Gikita. He tried to count the number of people he had killed but ran out of fingers. "Not knowing God, I did not live well," he mourned. Rachel noticed tears in his eyes.

Not long after that, Gikita testified that he was forgiven. Minkayi, the fifth killer, joined him, saying, "Believing, I am now walking Jesus' trail to the sky."

In the past months Betty and Rachel had learned more details of Palm Beach and why the Auca men had killed their loved ones. Now the killers, especially Uncle Gikita, were more able to talk about "the bad thing we did." With additional information, the two linguists were better able to piece the story together and understand something of the Auca's fear and hatred of foreigners that lay behind the attack.

Uncle Gikita said that Aucas had feared outsiders and

regarded them as the common enemy for longer than anyone could remember. A long time ago, before his grandfather's time, all the Aucas had lived far down the Napo River. Each time the foreigners came into the forest to chop trees, they grabbed a few more Aucas to eat. The Indians fled upriver, then later returned to their ancestral hunting grounds and took revenge, spearing more foreigners than they could count on their fingers and toes.

A bloody internal dispute that cost many lives had divided the tribe. Gikita's group fled farther upriver. But the foreigners kept coming. Some carried smoking sticks that could drop people in their tracks. The Indians learned to run when they heard the pop of a gun. Later they would follow the foreigners' trail back to their camp and wait until they became sleepy; then the Indians would rush in with spears flying.

The flying wood beetles with foreigners in their stomachs puzzled them the most. Some speculated that the souls of dead Aucas flew in the wood beetles. When one buzzed over, some climbed trees and others ran to the top of the highest hill to see where it was going. They always came back to say, "Flying it flew to the end of the blue where we could see it no more."

The yellow wood beetle that flew over in the fall of 1955 was the most mystifying of all. The foreigners in its stomach had yelled in the people's language, "We like you! We are Dayuma's friends!" and then dropped gifts. They liked the gifts, but it was the mention of Dayuma that electrified them. Night after night, they discussed her fate around the fires.

Dayuma's mother, Akawo, had always believed her to be alive and living somewhere with foreigners. What they heard from the wood beetle must be proof that this was so, she said. Some agreed with her, but others agreed that the foreigners had eaten Dayuma and the visitors in the wood beetle were only trying to trick her relatives into thinking she was alive.

Nampa, Dayuma's little brother, was sure that the foreigners in the wood beetle knew where his older sister was. "If they come again, I'm going to send them a parrot," he declared. He did.

Every flight increased Akawo's and Nampa's belief that the passengers in the wood beetle held the key to Dayuma's whereabouts. Perhaps Dayuma herself was even in the wood beetle's stomach. Nampa made a bamboo platform and announced that the next time the beetle came over and dropped a vine, he would climb up and see. But the rope broke and he tumbled back to the platform, deeply disappointed.

While the weekly flights continued, a more pressing matter was threatening the unity of the group. Naekiwi wanted Gimari, Dayuma's younger sister, for a second wife. But Mother Akawo opposed the marriage because it would cut across a cultural taboo that forbade the marriage of parallel cousins. A marriage between Naenkiwi and Gimari would violate this pattern.

Mother Akawo and Nampa had another reason for not wanting Gimari to move into Naenkiwi's hut. Naenkiwi had killed a man and kidnapped the man's daughter for his first wife. Then he took a second young girl from the hut of her protesting brother. Later, in a fit of anger, he had speared his first spouse. Now he wanted Gimari to replace her.

Unknown to Mother Akawo, Naenkiwi had arranged for the marriage to become official at a dance. While Akawo's attention was diverted, Naenkiwi's cohorts were to thrust him and Gimari into a hammock, the traditional way of pronouncing a couple married. Akawo discovered the plot and spirited her daughter away

Shell Mera, the mission base and home of Nate and Marj Saint, as seen from the air, with the runway in the middle of the picture.

Nate Saint as he appeared in 1946.

Marj Saint at her Shell Mera radio station.

From left to right, Ed McCully, Pete Fleming, and Jim Elliot with a parrot in Ecuador.

Roger Youderian with native Ecuadorian souvenirs.

Pete and Olive Fleming in Ecuador.

Fred and Clara Elliot with Jim, Betty, and baby Valerie in Ecuador in early 1955. That trip was the last time the senior Elliots saw Jim.

"George" – Naenkiwi – with a model plane on Palm Beach, shortly before the massacre.

On the right is the HCJB compound in downtown Quito, Ecuador. Most of the news of the massacre was relayed to the rest of the world by this missionary radio station.

The widows and their children, shortly after the massacre. The widows left to right: Betty Elliot, Barbara Youderian, Marj Saint, Olive Fleming (above), and Marilou McCully.

Dr. V. Raymond Edman, president of Wheaton College, baptized Dayuma, the first Auca believer, at the Wheaton Evangelical Free Church in 1958.

This shot was taken on the occasion of Dayuma's baptism. Left to right: Dr. Edman, Ed McCully's mother, Rachel Saint, Dayuma, Dayuma's son, Ignacio ("Sammy"), and Jim Elliot's parents.

Valerie Elliot and an Auca playmate, a few years after the massacre.

Rachel Saint was sometimes alone for months at a time while working with the Aucas. Her only link with the outside world was her radio.

Rachel checked Bible translation with many Auca helpers.

Don Johnson, director of Wycliffe in Ecuador, visits translator Catherine Peeke in Tiwaeno. Johnson was in the search party that buried the five martyrs on Palm Beach.

Minkayi, one of the Aucas who killed the martyrs and now a Christian.

Kimo, pilot Merrill Piper, and Gikita. Kimo and Gikita, two of the killers, are now both Christians.

Gikita, sitting in a missionary plane.

The Auca church building in Tiwaeno.

Easter Sunday 1965, the newly published gospel of Mark in Auca was dedicated in "God's speaking house." At left centre is Rachel Saint. To her left are Dayuma, Kimo, Phil Saint, and Don Johnson. Behind Rachel is Helen Johnson, and to Helen's left is Dawa.

Rachel with two proud parents, Dayuma and Komi, and their daughter.

A modern Auca family at home.

Barbara Youderian (right), one of the two widows still in Ecuador, welcomes a missionary guest arriving at the Gospel Missionary Union guest house in Quito.

A proud Auca grandmother.

Wycliffe plane Toña – named after the first Auca Christian martyr – on the ground at Tiwaeno.

ECUADOR

A LOS HEROES Y MARTIRES DEL ORIENTE ECUATORIANO

POR LA OFRENDA HEROICA Y LA EPOPEYA
INMORTAL DE SUS VIDAS AL SERVICIO
DE DIOS Y DE LA PATRIA EN LA
INCORPORACION DEL ORIENTE ECUATORIANO

TOÑA COBA M.

DOMINGO COMIN   AGUSTIN LEON
ALBINO DEL CURTO   SIMON HURTADO
JORGE ROSSI   PETER FLEMING
REBESCO SANTO   ROGER YOUDERIAN
ANTONIO DE LA VEGA   EDWARD MCCULLY
LUIS VELASQUEZ   JAMES ELLIOTT
MARIA DE LOS ANGELES AYESTERAN   NATHANIEL SAINT
MARIANO AZQUETA

EXMO Sr. PRESIDENTE DE LA   MINISTRO DE EDUCACION
REPUBLICA Dr.   Sr. Dr.
JOSE MARIA VELASCO IBARRA   FRANCISCO JARAMILLO DAVILA

LIMONCOCHA, FEBRERO 12 DE 1972

This monument was built by the Ecuadorian government in Limoncocha to honour Catholic and evangelical martyrs. The name of Toña, the first Auca Christian martyr, is at top centre, and the names of the five Americans are on the right.

Photos provided by: James Hefley, Cheri Hefley, Merrill Piper, MAF, and others.

the night of the dance. Furious at being thwarted, Naenkiwi threatened to kill Akawo and Nampa if they wouldn't let Gimari marry him.

Gimari herself was infatuated with Naenkiwi, but she didn't want her mother and brother killed.

One day the yellow wood beetle circled just above the treetops. "Come to the Curaray!" a voice invited. "We want to visit you. Come! We will meet you there." The wood beetle flew off in the direction of the big river that ran through the southern part of Auca territory.

Later that day, some of the men were hunting near the Curaray and heard chopping. They followed the sound to the river's edge. Peeking from the jungle, they saw the wood beetle resting on the sand and several foreigners nearby. They hurried back to tell the others.

Gimari and Aunt Mintaka slipped away at daybreak the next morning to see the foreigners. Naenkiwi discovered what had happened and ran to bring Gimari back. "No," she told him when he caught up, "I'm going to the foreigners to find out about Dayuma." Unable to persuade her otherwise, he decided to accompany her and Mintaka to the Curaray. Nearing the river, they heard a foreign voice calling in their language, "We are friends. We have come to visit you."

The three stopped to listen. "I'm going across," Gimari declared.

"No," Naenkiwi objected, "they have smoking sticks and will kill us."

"I'm going," Gimari announced, and stepped into the water. Mintaka followed, then Naenkiwi.

The auburn-headed foreigner (Jim) who had been shouting phrases splashed through the water to meet them. He grabbed their hands and led them to the beach, jabbering words they could not understand. Four other foreigners waited on the beach, including the short-haired one (Nate) they had always noticed in the wood beetle's stomach.

As the foreigners clustered around them, gesturing and jabbering, the Aucas could only comprehend "friends" and "welcome." Naenkiwi they called "George" and Gimari "Delilah," but neither knew what this meant.

Gimari lost no time in speaking her wishes. "Take me to my sister, Dayuma," she pleaded. "I want to go to Dayuma."

The foreigners looked blank. "Don't you understand?" Mintaka broke in. "She wants to go with you in the wood beetle to see Dayuma. She is Dayuma's sister."

Gimari stroked the plane and rubbed her naked body against it. "Please take me to Dayuma," she begged. "I want to see my sister." They still did not understand.

The foreigners passed out gifts: knives and a machete. The short-haired one took a little wood beetle made from sticks and tried to show them what would happen if it tried to come down in trees.

Naenkiwi kept looking at the big wood beetle. The short-haired one pointed inside and Naenkiwi smiled. The foreigner helped Naenkiwi into the wood beetle's stomach, then he climbed in on the other side. Up and over the trees they soared; then the wood beetle sat down again on the beach.

Naenkiwi sat still. The short-hair took this to mean he wanted another ride. This time they flew in the wood beetle over the clearing. Naenkiwi smiled at the familiar faces. He cheered and shouted, anticipating that he would be the talk of all the clearing. He had flown in a wood beetle.

When the wood beetle sat down on the beach, Naenkiwi jumped out, clapping his hands. The foreigners beamed and lifted their heads, talking to the sky. The Aucas looked on in puzzlement. Foreigners were so strange.

What wonders the foreigners displayed: little vines that stretched (rubber bands), fish bladders that swelled as big as a man's head when air was puffed into them (balloons), a drink so sweet it hurt your teeth (lemonade), and delicious meat jammed between a kind of soft manioc (hamburgers).

After eating, Naenkiwi put his machete and other gifts in the wood beetle's stomach. The short-haired one shook his head and handed the things back to Naenkiwi. Then he and the foreigner with big eyes (Pete wore glasses) got in the wood beetle and flew away.

Gimari's eyes followed the wood beetle as it buzzed above the trees. "Why wouldn't they take me to Dayuma?" she moaned. "Is it because they have already killed and eaten her? I'm leaving." She whirled and stalked off down the beach. Naenkiwi thought she was running away and shouted, "Gimari! Come back!" When she paid no attention to his calls, he ran after her into the forest.

Mintaka remained on the beach, thinking the foreigners might take her to Dayuma. The foreigners kept saying "We like you," but they never said a word about Dayuma. When darkness fell, they climbed up into their tree house. She built a fire and stayed on the beach most of the night, hoping the foreigners would come down and at least provide some information about her niece. Shortly before daybreak, she gave up and left.

On the trail back to the clearing, Naenkiwi and Gimari had met her mother, brother, and younger sisters on the way to the river. "We were coming to join you at the foreigners' camp," Akawo said.

Naenkiwi scowled. "The foreigners will only kill you.

They tried to kill us."

"It is true," Gimari lied. "The foreigners tried to kill us."

Disappointed, Akawo and her other children walked back to the clearing and found others preparing to visit the foreigners. Akawo reported what Naenkiwi and Gimari had said. Maengamo, wife of Uncle Gikita, challenged the story. "How do we know they're telling the truth? Naenkiwi lies all the time. They may be good foreigners. Didn't they drop us good things?

"They are young. I am old. I will go and join Mintaka on the river and see for myself." But the sun was sinking, and Maengamo was persuaded to remain with the group.

Naenkiwi and Gimari came into the clearing. Naenkiwi repeated what they had told Gimari's family on the trail. He surveyed the men sitting around their huts. "What will you do about these foreigners who tried to kill us?" he demanded. He waited for an answer, a smirk on his face. "Well, if you aren't brave enough, I'll kill them myself."

Gimari hung close to him, drawing frowns from her mother and brother. "She is going to be my wife," Naenkiwi declared.

Akawo shouted back her disapproval. Naenkiwi glared at her defiantly. They exchanged more words. Naenkiwi saw others beginning to get angry. Suddenly he ran into his house and came out with spears and a machete. He started toward Gikita's hut, figuring that if he killed the old man, the rest would not prevent him from taking Gimari.

His sister Minimo, wife of Dayuma's half-brother Minkayi, grabbed him by the throat and screamed. Gimari's cousin Nimonga and Uncle Gikita ran out and held him. Others broke his spears and took his machete

"Why spear Uncle Gikita?" Nimonga yelled. "Why don't you just ask for my cousin and take her without killing? Go with her," he said in disgust.

"No!" Mother Akawo screamed. "They cannot marry." Akawo grabbed Gimari protectively.

Young Nampa pulled his sister away and shoved her toward Naenkiwi. "Take her and go to the foreigners and live."

"The foreigners will only kill us," Naenkiwi insisted. "They killed Dayuma and the other Auca girls who went to the outside. They beat us on the beach and tried to kill us with machetes."

Old Maengamo jumped into the verbal battle. "He lies. They are good foreigners, I say. With them we will live well. They will not hurt us. I will join Mintaka on the beach."

"They are bad! Bad!" Naenkiwi yelled back. "I'll go myself and kill them all." Snatching Gimari by the arm, he ran with her into the forest.

"Don't try to come back to your hammock," Akawo screamed at her daughter. "Never!"

The frustrations and hostilities felt over the internal quarrel aggravated feelings about the foreigners. As the shadows darkened into night, Gikita and the younger men sat by their fires and recalled all they knew about outsiders. They finally reached a consensus that the foreigners on the Curaray were bad. Naenkiwi and Gimari had been there and must have told the truth.

Then Mintaka returned the next morning and refuted what Naenkiwi and Gimari had said. "They are really good foreigners," she reported. "They laughed a lot and gave us gifts. They never tried to harm any of us."

The men were whittling spears furiously, too inflamed to be convinced. Gikita was spurring them on: "If we don't kill them, they will kill and eat us. Make many spears. There are five now, but more may come. Hurry!"

The scent of battle was in the old man's nostrils. For years he had wanted to repay his downriver enemies for spearing members of his family. To do that he needed some trained warriors. Tomorrow on the Curaray, the young ones in his upriver group would taste blood for the first time. This would prepare them for the more important battle.

The sun climbed in the sky and the yellow beetle buzzed over again. The men remained in their huts, making spears. The women ran to hide as a foreigner called, "Come to the Curaray. Come. We are your friends." They dropped more gifts.

The wood beetle came back a short while later. This time the men came out smiling. The foreigners waved and called cordialities, not knowing that they had already been sentenced to die.

The next day (Sunday, January 8), when the sun was high, the men finished whittling their spears. "Let's go," shouted Uncle Gikita. "Yes, let's go," young voices echoed. Nimonga, Minkayi, Dyuwi, and Kimo got in step behind their leader. Mintaka; Mother Akawo; Minkayi's wife, Minimo; Kimo's wife, Dawa; and young Nampa trotted farther back.

The crafty Naenkiwi, who had boasted that he would kill the foreigners if the others didn't, was not in the war party. He and Gimari were hiding somewhere in the forest.

"Spearing, we will kill the foreigners at the river," the warriors chanted. "We will separate their souls from their skins." Their voices drowned out the plea of Gikita's wife, Maengamo, not to kill.

"They are good foreigners. They come to do us no harm," she kept repeating. "Let them live in peace."

The war party hurried on, oblivious to her cries.

Far down the trail, they heard the buzz of the wood beetle again. Squinting into the sun, they saw the plane pass overhead on its final trip over the clearing.

They reached the river's edge around midafternoon. By prearranged plan, the five men hid in dense undergrowth while the three women and Nampa waded openhanded into the river.

The foreigners saw them and called, "Welcome! Welcome!" The women smiled. Nampa moved to one side and maneuvered to get behind the plane.

By gesturing, Mintaka got two of the foreigners to follow her up the beach, Minimo persuaded two others to follow her in the other direction. Akawo stayed with the fifth at the cooking fire.

The rattle of spears from across the river caught the ear of the foreigner beside the fire. Akawo saw him reach for his gun and tried to snatch the weapon away. As they struggled, Nampa ran from his hiding spot on the far side of the plane. The gun went off, the bullet grazing Nampa's head.

The four younger Auca men hesitated in fear. "Come on! Come on!" Gikita shouted. "Spear the foreigners before they kill us!"

The foreigners downstream and upstream were not shooting at all. Spear upraised, Gikita ran toward the one who was trying to fight Akawo off. The foreigner thrust his hands upward, spouting words Gikita could not understand. Gikita threw the spear. The foreigner staggered and fell into the water. Gikita hurled another spear and another until satisfied that his victim was dead.

Dyuwi, Kimo, Nimonga, and Minkayi were chasing the other foreigners along the beach. Gikita ran to help them. One reached the wood beetle, climbed inside, and fired his smoking stick into the air. Then, to the surprise of the attackers, he jumped out and ran back to help his friends. An Auca speared him from behind and he fell mortally wounded into the water.

When the spearing was done, the Aucas attacked the wood beetle, beating its body with rocks, stripping the skin from inside its stomach. Then they climbed into the tree house and threw out the foreigner's possessions. Their fury spent, Gikita looked over the bloody scene with satisfaction. "It is done," he said. "Spearing, you did well," he told the young men.

They met Dabu on the trail leading home. He had been away from the clearing and had not known of their mission. "I am going to invite the foreigners to my house," he said.

"They are dead," Gikita announced. "We speared them and smashed their wood beetle."

Dabu had not been taken in by Naenkiwi's and Gimari's falsehoods. "Why did you kill them?" he shouted in anger. "Did they hurt you?"

"Naenkiwi and Gimari said they were bad and tried to kill them."

Dabu shook with rage. "Naenkiwi and Gimari told you wrong. You have speared foreigners who came in peace."

> *"And the contention was so sharp between*
> *[Paul and Barnabas], that they departed*
> *asunder."*
> Acts 15:39, KJV

The Parting 7

"The president is coming and wants to meet some Aucas," came the summons from Limoncocha.

Rachel selected Dayuma, Kimo, and Dawa to meet Ecuador's chief executive. Traveling on foot and by canoe to Arajuno, they were picked up by a plane and flown to the jungle center just ahead of two government planes arriving from Quito. President Velasco Ibarra and his immediate entourage were on the first plane. The second carried twenty more officials and Uncle Cam Townsend, who had left Charlotte, North Carolina, immediately upon hearing the news.

"I've prayed for five years that God would give me the privilege of introducing one of the men who killed your brother to the president of Ecuador," Townsend reminded Rachel. "That prayer is about to be answered."

An afternoon outdoor ceremony had been planned involving the government officials and representatives of the tribes with which SIL was working in Ecuador. A heavy downpour caused cancellation of the formal affair, but Velasco Ibarra didn't seem to mind. His primary reason in coming was to meet Aucas.

Five years before, he had presented his country's National Medal of Merit to Abe Van Der Puy, who received the award on behalf of the five missionaries slain on Palm Beach. Later the president was amazed to learn that the wife of one and the sister of another of the martyrs had gone to live with the legendary Aucas. Now he was going to the house of Don and Helen Johnson—which had been spruced up to serve as the presidential suite—to meet one of the transformed killers.

Rachel and Dayuma led Kimo and Dawa into the house, where a beaming Uncle Cam was waiting to make the introductions.

"Mr. President, may I present Miss Rachel Saint. You met her several years ago when our group came to your residence to offer our services to your ministry of education. And this is Dayuma, the young Auca woman Miss Saint found working on a hacienda. And—"

Kimo suddenly stepped forward and rubbed his broad hand across the presidential bald pate! Uncle Cam suppressed a smile. Rachel turned red. "Please excuse him, Mr. President," she blurted in apology. "He must have been trying to brush off a fly."

"I think he's never seen a bald head," Uncle Cam ventured. "He had to find out if it was real."

Everyone laughed. "Don't be embarrassed, Miss Saint," Ibarra assured. "Please be comfortable." Kimo and Dawa squatted, flat-footed, on the floor. Dayuma settled on a low stool nearby to keep a watchful eye on both.

The president wanted to know how the contact had been made and how Rachel and Betty had pacified the killers. "Mr. President, we give all credit to God," Rachel said. "He arranged the circumstances for us to enter." She noted the seeming providence in that the five men had made the gift drops to Dayuma's family instead of to the hostile downriver group. The constantly changing beach on which they landed had never been that long before or afterward. A plane could not land there now. When Mintaka and Maengamo came out of the jungle, the Aucas were living closer to the outside world than they had in the seven years of Dayuma's absence.

"You say this man Kimo was one of those who killed the missionaries," the president said, interrupting, "and that he and the other four have stopped killing? How did that happen?"

When Rachel mentioned changed hearts. he asked in puzzlement, "How do you teach such people about God?"

"Mr. President," Rachel said, "the same message serves for all people, everywhere; the message of forgiveness and faith in Jesus, God's Son, changes hearts."

Ibarra looked at Kimo, who still squatted on the floor, gazing around in wonderment. "What can this man here comprehend about God?"

"Mr. President, why don't you ask Kimo, and I will interpret for you."

"Very well. 'Kimo, who is Jesus Christ?' "

When Rachel translated, Kimo brightened. "Jesus Christ is the One who came from heaven and died for my sins. He made me stop killing, and now I live happily with my brothers."

"Amazing!" the president exclaimed when Rachel gave this back. "Amazing!"

That night, at a dinner banquet given by the.Wycliffe group for the president and his party, Ibarra was still talking about the change in Kimo. "Mr. President," Uncle Cam assured him, "we see this happen again and again when primitive tribesmen hear the Word of God in their own language. Perhaps you can understand why we are so eager to help the jungle Indians?"

"Yes, of course, Uncle Cam. Where will you be going next?"

"To Peru, for the graduation exercises of the bilingual teachers at our jungle center. Then to visit our work in Brazil."

"Brazil, you say. Janio Quadros, the new president, is a friend of mine. If you'd like to see him, I can have my ambassador set up an appointment."

"I'd be most grateful, Mr. President."

"And now perhaps you can do me a favor? Do you know the famous evangelist Billy Graham?"

"Yes, we are friends. He approves of our work."

"Well, I've been hearing a lot about him. Do you think he might come to Quito and preach for us?"

"I'll certainly ask him," Townsend promised. "I'm sure he'll pray about coming and will seek God's will."

"Good. Good. I thank you and your staff for their good work. My government will continue to stand behind you. Imagine, Aucas that have stopped killing and teach the Bible! Amazing! I never would have believed it."

Ibarra kept his word. Uncle Cam saw the Brazilian president and was able to explain Wycliffe's program there. "How can I help?" the Brazilian asked. When presented with a list of requests, he declared, "I will do it."

With the conversion of the killers, the Aucas built houses for Betty and Rachel. The roofs were palm thatch like the Auca dwellings, but the houses included such luxuries as split-palm floors, screens, tables, and chairs, and a separate bedroom for Val.

The Aucas wanted to end their isolation and began felling trees and digging out deep-rooted stumps to make a 600-foot landing strip adjacent to the settlement beside the Tiwaeno River. SIL pilots had monitored the progress while making supply drops to the linguists. In April 1961, Don Smith thought the strip was service-

able. "Whenever you think it's safe," he told Rachel
and Betty.

They kept thinking of the Palm Beach killings and the
mutilated plane. Had the gospel penetrated deep
enough in Auca culture to permit another plane to land?
The women weighed the risks and finally decided to
give Smith the go-ahead.

The Aucas watched in wonder as the plane slipped
down over the trees and touched the ground. Rachel
and Betty heard no threat and saw no spears wielded.
They wished that Nate, Jim, Ed, Pete, and Roger could
have seen this day.

Before Don took off, they had a brief dedication of the
strip. "Our God in heaven," Dyuwi prayed, "we thank
you for bringing this day when our people and outsiders can meet in peace." Then the pilot taxied into
position, revved his engine, and roared into the sky.

Tiwaeno was only a ten-minute flight from Arajuno
and civilization, twenty minutes from Shell Mera, a half
hour from Limoncocha. Days of brutal hiking over nar-
row trails with the risk of being bitten by poisonous
snakes or attacked by hostile Indians were now reduced
to minutes.

Progress in language analysis now took an upward
turn. In May 1961, the SIL plane picked up Kimo and
Minkayi and their wives along with Rachel and Dayuma
for a linguistic workshop at Limoncocha under the
direction of Dr. Kenneth Pike. At this time, Wycliffe's
top linguist officially approved the Auca alphabet that
Rachel and Betty had produced and gave the formal
go-ahead for translation of the gospel of Mark.

An old friend of Rachel's came to Tiwaeno to devote
the summer to helping with the translation. Slim and
very soft-spoken, Catherine Peeke was still waiting for
her tribal assignment. She and Mary Sargent had

planned to work with Ecuadorian Zaparos but had
found only ten who could speak the ancestral language.
Cathy, as everyone called her, was now serving as
director of technical studies for all the SIL workers in
Ecuador. Recognizing the brilliance of this quiet country
girl from the North Carolina mountains, Wycliffe leaders had also encouraged her to pursue a doctorate in
linguistics at the University of Indiana and do her dissertation on Auca grammar.

Cathy had attended the Summer Institute of Linguistics course at the University of Oklahoma the summer
Jim Elliot was there. She had come to Ecuador before
the five men were killed. Since she had known Betty
and Rachel longer than most missionaries, she understood their incompatabilities.

Indeed, the gap between Rachel and Betty had grown
wider. Years of living among the Aucas and seeing each
other constantly had not brought the two highly motivated women any closer. Aware of the emotional distance between them, Cathy tried to be a friend to both.

Translating Scripture into the difficult Auca language
was tough enough. Because of their long isolation from
the world, the Aucas had no concepts of buying and
selling, sowing and reaping of grain, or words for
carpenter or *teacher*. They were unfamiliar with camels,
donkeys, cattle, sheep, grapevines, and wine. They did
not use grinding stones or stones in building. Market-
places and political boundaries were unknown. Divisions between rich and poor and relationships between
servants and master and teachers and learners were
completely foreign to their thinking.

In many instances, the translators could only look for
a verbal form that conveyed the meaning of the biblical
term. Thus *disciple* became ''one who lives following
Jesus.'' Even here the translators had to use a different

form for a disciple going and one coming.

They could find no absolute superlative in Auca. For "the smallest of all seeds" it was necessary to say, "There is no such tiny seed like this anywhere."

For the rebuking of the waves on the Sea of Galilee by Jesus, it was necessary to complete one process in Auca before tending to the other. So they rendered: "Jesus then said, 'Why ever (does the) wind blow, for goodness' sake?'

"Then it became not blowing.

" 'Water quiet down, don't do it!' He said. Then the water quickly quieted down and it was not doing anything."

There was no way to say with a single verb that both the wind and the water were calm.

They had to be careful of the conclusions that Aucas might draw from a biblical incident. For instance, when they were reading aloud about Herodias's asking Herod for the head of John the Baptist on a platter, Dawa remarked, "They must have been cannibals."

They came to the verse that said, "They spit on Jesus." "How do you act when you're mad?" Rachel asked the group. "Do you ever spit on people?"

The Aucas sitting around all said "No." Then Kimo spoke up and said, "We don't, but that's what the jaguar does when he's mad. He goes t-t-t—" and Kimo spat in the air.

They came to where the scribes shook their heads. "When you get disgusted with someone, do you shake your head?"

Again they answered "No." Again Kimo spoke up. "That's what the jaguar does, only he wags his tail, like this," and he waved his hand back and forth to indicate how the jaguar wagged his tail.

Cathy Peeke flew out in August, leaving Betty and

Rachel to continue the slow, tedious translation work. Every word, phrase, and grammatical form had to be checked with Dayuma or someone else. Rachel's habit was to write out a trial verse by herself, then read it to Dayuma and ask her questions to amplify the meaning. There was always the problem of grammar. In one instance, Rachel used the right suffixes with the wrong stem. Dayuma looked at her and asked, "Did Jesus put John in jail?" Dayuma knew better, of course, but she wanted Rachel to know that the translation was incorrect.

Progress was slow because so much time was consumed in doing all the chores necessary for living in a primitive situation. The two women were also doctor and nurse. The Aucas were astoundingly healthy as primitive people go, but one came to Betty or Rachel almost every day with an ailment that she was supposed to fix. Each had a medical kit and could handle routine problems. More difficult cases had to be called in to Dr. Everett Fuller, the missionary medic at the HCJB-related hospital in Shell Mera. Critical emergencies required an airlift to the hospital.

The medical pioneer among the jungle Indians of eastern Ecuador, Dr. Fuller had personally known each of the five martyrs and with great interest had followed developments among the Aucas. One morning, after discussing a patient over the radio, he mentioned that he would soon be leaving for special surgical studies in Panama. "Before I go, I'd count it a privilege to fly out and hold a clinic," he said.

Dayuma had been eager for the new believers to "enter the water." Upon hearing that Dr. Fuller was coming, she immediately announced that he would perform the baptisms. SIL personnel refrained from officiating at religious ceremonies. The linguists counseled that no one should feel pressure and asked those who wished to "enter the water" as Jesus had to come privately and say so.

Wycliffe's Forrest Zander flew Dr. Fuller in on Thanksgiving morning, just a little over three years after Betty's and Rachel's entry. Dr. Fuller treated snakebites, sutured machete wounds, and gave shots in the morning, then Dayuma called the group together for the baptismal service. With Rachel and Dayuma interpreting, Dr. Fuller explained that baptism signified a complete break with the old life and a determination to follow Jesus in every respect. Then he waded into the cool waters of the stream that ran near the airstrip and immersed nine while the rest looked on from the rocky beach. Those who "entered the water to follow Jesus" included Dawa, the first convert inside Auca territory, and her husband, Kimo; Oba, Dayuma's sister, and her husband, Dyuwi; Gikita, Dayuma's uncle, and his son, Komi; Nimonga; Gimari, Dayuma's sister, and Ipa, both widows of "George" of Palm Beach.

Rachel wrote: "For me—one who has watched the expression of Auca faces turn from resentment to friendship, from unbelief to belief—the biggest blessing was to see the sweet radiance of their faces as they came up from the waters. Our hearts rejoiced in this answer to the sacrifice and the prayers of many people."

The reports that all five killers were now believers and four had been baptized made sensational news among evangelicals abroad and brought a new wave of journalists, Christian tourists, and preachers to Ecuador. Some of the ministers claimed they were following the call of God to hold a Bible conference or evangelistic crusade among the Aucas and wished to charter a plane to Tiwaeno. Their missionary contacts referred them to Wycliffe leaders, who patiently explained why the Aucas were not ready for a flood of visitors.

One whom they did welcome to Tiwaeno was Dave Howard, who came for a week. Then Rachel's missionary brother Phil arrived with his movie camera to make a film about the converted killers. Dayuma scheduled another baptismal service. Among those immersed this time were Minkayi, the fifth killer, and Tona, an extremely bright young Indian who years before had fled with his mother from the downriver group after his father had been speared. His commitment to Christ had not come easily. For months he glared at Rachel and Betty with hatred instilled in him from past clashes with outsiders. His prejudices slowly melted, and one Sunday he responded to Dayuma's invitation to accept Christ.

Phil Saint titled his forty-minute film *I Saw Aucas Pray*. The leaflets distributed to thousands of churches and Christian organizations in the U.S. exemplified the kind of publicity appearing about the conversion of the Palm Beach killers.

> I stood on Palm Beach with the savage who killed my brother Nate—he is a killer no longer. I lived in an Auca village and saw with my own eyes the marvelous change God has wrought there in the jungle!
>
> Watch Aucas on the screen! See up close the Auca hunters using blowguns, and fishing with spears. Feel the power and majesty of the great rain forest. Hear the weird chants of those forgotten jungle dwellers. . . . All this and more! See the power of the Gospel of Christ!
>
> Thousands have been waiting for word of Aucas being saved and transformed. At last the care-

fully documented facts have been made available
for all to see and hear. It is a thrilling story of
savage fear and hate conquered by God's message
of divine love and forgiveness. Heathen supersti-
tions have been driven from many hearts as
"God's Carving" (The Bible) has been taught.

The leaflets also featured pictures of Rachel "living
and working among those who killed her brother."
There was no mention of Betty, who believed that the
Aucas were being exploited in missionary promotion
and becoming a circus display for the gratification of
American evangelicals.

Betty was also bothered by some writers' claims that
God had allowed the five men to be killed so that the
Aucas might be saved. That might be part of His purpose, she conceded, but who was wise enough to dis-
cern the whole pattern? God's ways were past finding
out.

Rachel saw the publicity as a means of communicating what God could do when primitive people were
given the gospel and God's Word in their own language. She was puzzled by Betty's objections. Hadn't
she written *Through Gates of Splendor* and consented to
the first film on the death of the five martyrs? Wasn't
that missionary promotion? And wasn't the salvation of
many Aucas evidence that the five had not died in vain?

Auca stories kept rolling off the presses. Every Christian magazine wanted an update, and travelers to Auca
land were asked for write-ups of their visits. One of the
most touching reports came from Ed McCully's father.
He wrote for *Action*, the official journal of the National
Association of Evangelicals:

I wanted personally to let the five Stone Age sav-

ages know that I loved them, not for their cruel
deed of savagery, but because God loved them and
these five soldiers of the cross loved them enough
to give up their own lives.

T. E. McCully came with Barbara Youderian, his
daughter-in-law Marilou, and his grandson Matt. As
they climbed out of the plane, Betty and Valerie (now a
charming seven-year-old) came to greet them. When
T. E. kissed them, the Aucas laughed. Betty quickly explained that kissing was not in their culture.

T. E. had his picture taken with the five killers. Then
he threw his arms around each and delivered the message he had come so far to bring: "I love you."

The Aucas were most impressed with the size of their
guest. Gikita measured his foot alongside the American's. Kimo asked him to remove his belt to see how it
might fit them. When Kimo discovered that he and
another man could easily get inside it, they cackled with
laughter.

T. E. watched the killers of his son laughing and talking with Betty and Rachel. He wrote: "It is hard to imagine these men as killers of the five missionaries—men
who put the spears through your own son who had
brought joy to your heart for 28 years. Yet I realized
afresh that God is infinitely wise and therefore He cannot err. He is omnipotent and therefore nothing can
take place without His permission."

Barbara and Marilou caught Betty up on the latest
news. Marilou and Marj Saint were going to the States
in a few months with their children for a year's furlough. In Marilou's absence, Barbara would be leaving
the jungle to take over the children's home in Quito.
Beth was now eleven and Jerry nine. She had taught
them at the mission station and felt it was time they

began studying at the Alliance's Christian academy with others their age.

Betty asked about Olive, who she knew had married Dr. Walter Liefeld about a year before. "We have good news. They have a son named David."

These visitors left. Others came and went. Betty and Rachel continued their work, so near physically and yet so far apart in other ways.

Betty recognized the problems in their relationship, but she hoped to remain with the Aucas at least a few more years. However, it soon became apparent to Betty that the difficulties between them were too great to overcome.

The die was cast and Betty began packing. She did not try to explain why she was leaving to Val or to the Aucas, nor did Rachel. The Aucas had seen their beloved Gikari and her little daughter leave before, and they had always come back. Betty did not tell them that she had no idea when or where she would see them again. They would not understand.

She gave her language files, the results of years of work, to Cathy Peeke, who would become Rachel's permanent partner after finishing doctoral studies. Betty and Val moved back to the house Jim had built in Shandia. They remained there about a year, with Betty teaching Val as she had in Tiwaeno and working with the Quichuas. Finally, Betty felt it was time for her to leave Ecuador for good and continue her writing ministry in the United States. She moved to Franconia, New Hampshire, where she enrolled Val in school and began writing her first novel. *No Graven Image* was a bittersweet story about a young, idealistic missionary named Margaret Sparhawk who came to the Quichua Indians of Ecuador with great expectations and saw all her hopes dashed. Eventually she was left only with God's promise: "I am with thee."

Unlike her previous books, which had sold many thousands of copies and made her one of the best-known names in American evangelicalism, *No Graven Image* was not well-received by the majority of her fellow believers. Many called the book a disappointment, a poor reflection of missionary life, a dishonor to God. Others praised her for daring to be realistic and said they were glad somebody of Betty Elliot's stature finally had the courage to tell about the dark valleys of the soul that many missionaries faced. A few suggested there were more Margaret Sparhawks on the mission field than most people believed.

Betty's books had made her so well-known and her reputation as a writer was so well-established that she could easily begin a new career of writing and speaking. Everywhere she was asked about the Aucas and why she had left. Over and over she said, "Part of the reason is that I needed to get Valerie into school. The other part is personal, which I'd rather not discuss."

"I trust the Aucas' Christianity. It isn't just something to do. It cost them something."
Kathy Saint

The Saints and the Indians 8

Betty Elliot's departure left Rachel and Cathy Peeke solely responsible for linguistic analysis and translation of the Bible into Auca. With Barbara Youderian now in Quito, the last of the five widows had departed from the jungle in which they had once intended to spend their lives.

The evangelical world, however, would forever connect them with the Aucas. Barbara, settled into the children's home in Quito, was besieged by Christian tourists. In the homeland, Betty, though recognized as a writer in her own right, was "Jim Elliot's widow." Olive, with a new husband, name, and child, was sought out for speaking engagements about the Aucas. Marilou and Marj, living next door to each other during their furlough year in New Jersey, also had more invitations to speak than they could handle. Every audience wanted to hear two things: a remembrance of Palm Beach and a current report on the Aucas.

The widows in the States left a large part of their hearts in Ecuador, where their loved ones were buried and where they had so many missionary friends. While in New Jersey, Marilou and Marj were saddened to hear that one of their dearest friends, Delores Van Der Puy, had incurable bone cancer. The Van Der Puys and

Saints had been especially close. Abe was the one to tell Marj, in 1948, that Nate had been seriously injured in an accident near the Quito airport. When the search was on for Nate and his friends in Auca territory, Abe went to Shell Mera to write the news releases that kept families and the world informed. After Marj came to take over the HCJB guest house in Quito, the Van Der Puys were like second parents to the Saint children.

"Not Dee!" was both Marilou's and Marj's reaction when they heard the news. They prayed that God would perform a miracle and, if this was not His will, that He would give her grace to bear the pain and give Abe and the children the strength to carry on. Having lost loved ones themselves, Marilou and Marj could identify with the suffering, but they felt that seeing a loved one die slowly and being unable to help would be harder than a sudden loss.

Meanwhile, life went on for Rachel and the Aucas in Tiwaeno. Cathy was still away working on her doctorate, leaving Rachel without a partner. Rachel could not leave; she felt needed too much. The translation had to go on. Not even when her father died, at age eighty-four, did she feel free to go home. She knew that he was in heaven. That was what counted.

Almost eight years had passed since Palm Beach, almost six since the entry into the tribe. Rachel had watched Auca children grow into young manhood and womanhood. For the first time in the tribe's history, marriages between Christians were in the offing.

Young Tona and Wato were the first. Tona, the former rebel from downriver, was fast becoming one of the most exemplary believers in the group. Wato, when a child, had lost her father in a spearing raid and her mother to kidnappers. She had been raised by Uncle Gikita and was also a Christian.

The traditional wedding party lasted four nights. The men donned their best feathers and gallop-danced around the clearing and airstrip, waving palm fronds and chanting the ancestral songs. The women joined hands and swayed rhythmically together, babies bouncing in back slings at their mothers' sides. Children formed groups of their own and danced about, chanting and chattering as they, too, became caught up in the excitement.

On the fourth night, several young men picked up Tona, galloped with him to the hammock where Wato was sitting, and plopped him down beside her. Behind them came the old women, to offer the traditional advice.

Dayuma was determined not to let the opportunity pass. Stepping before the happy couple, she announced, "God's Carving says, 'They two shall be one flesh." Everyone quieted down as she quoted from Scripture, then she turned to Rachel and asked, "Who is to pray?" Rachel pointed to Kimo, and he asked that they would walk in God's ways.

The next wedding was Dayuma's. As a young widow on Carlos Sevilla's hacienda, she had come close to marrying another Quichua; it was good that she had waited. Now she was to be joined to Komi, the handsome son of Gikita and Maengamo. They were cousins, but their marriage was in the proper kinship pattern.

Pilot Don Smith was the special guest of honor. He galloped with the men in the traditional wedding dance. When they dumped Komi in Dayuma's hammock, he squatted beside them as they said, "Now you are married!" Then he asked God's blessing on the union, and they went to Rachel's house for wedding cake and canned peach halves. When Komi tried to eat with a spoon, everyone convulsed with laughter.

Kimo's house was becoming too crowded for the Sunday morning services. He proposed that they build a special house for worship. "God's speaking-house" was constructed large enough to accommodate the entire group. It had the traditional thatched roof supported by long corner poles, with a split-palm-platform floor about four feet off the ground. The platform was to keep out the goats and geese that Rachel had imported to supplement the group's food supply. There was also a stair of notched poles for the convenience of visitors. The Aucas preferred to shinny up the big corner poles.

When the sanctuary was finished, the Aucas assembled for worship at about sunup on the following Sunday. The men and boys occupied one side of the platform, the women and girls the other. *"Waengongi badonke inonae,"* they chanted. "All this sphere is God's creation."

Dayuma, radiant in a rose-colored sundress, moved to the center. She sat facing the women but spoke mostly to the men, who grunted the equivalent of *amen* at appropriate times, while wiggly children and nursing mothers were a little less attentive.

For the lesson, Dayuma ticked off the Ten Commandments, with direct applications to such unholy practices as "laughing with another's spouse," which could lead to adultery, and choking unwanted infants to death. "We may kill animals," she said, "but not imperfect children. God has given them into our care."

When Dayuma finished, Rachel glanced knowingly at Kimo. He gave a long, rambling discourse on the parable of the good Samaritan. Then Dyuwi pronounced the benediction, and Sunday worship was over.

As the Aucas' knowledge of the Bible increased, so did their concern for their downriver enemy kinsmen. News came of the spearing of two Quichuas and the capture of a small girl on the Napo River. Hunters from Tiwaeno discovered footprints only a day's walk away that they thought belonged to downriver scouts. Were downriver warriors planning an attack on Tiwaeno? The Christian Aucas implored God to show them a way to reach their hostile downriver relatives before there was bloodshed.

One Sunday morning in November 1963, Dyuwi spoke up after the first song. "Last night, God told me to go to the unbelievers downriver."

"They'll spear you," someone cried.

"God sending me, I will go," Dyuwi declared. "If I die, my soul will go to God's house. Then He will send someone else, as He sent His messengers to us after we speared the five foreigners."

More weeks passed. The possibility of an attack by downriver people still loomed. Dyuwi was warned again, but he was not to be swayed.

"Jesus told us, 'Two by two, two by two, we should go,' " the young Auca reminded the group on another Sunday. Gikita responded by praying aloud, "God, if you say to me, 'Go,' then I will go. If you say, 'Stay,' I will stay."

Day after day they discussed the missionary venture. Rachel recognized the dangers and recalled that God had opened the way to the upriver group by sending Dayuma to the outside. "Let us pray that God will send someone to us from the downriver people," she suggested.

SIL pilots had been flying the "safe" route from Limoncocha, following the Napo River, then heading directly into Tiwaeno instead of taking the shorter route, which required flying over territory of the hostile downriver Aucas. Aware that the Auca believers were now talking of a missionary journey downriver, pilot

Merrill Piper took the shortcut and spotted several clearings.

In January 1964, downriver Aucas attacked settlers living along the Napo. Hearing that more outsiders were moving into Auca territory, Dabu, Kimo's brother, asked SIL personnel to warn them to keep out or they would be killed. "Before we heard God's Carving, we killed outsiders who came into our territory," he recalled.

To make the situation more difficult, oil activity had picked up. Some promising finds had been made near the Napo, in the hunting territory of the downriver Aucas. Prospects looked so good that twenty-seven oil companies, including Texaco and Gulf, were working in the area.

Dayuma was worried about the future of her group. Having lived in the outside, she knew that the oil workers would build roads that would bring more settlers seeking land. The territorial rights claimed by her people would mean nothing. She tried to convey the threat to the others, along with her hope that a large tract in the Tiwaeno area could be set aside, and that there upriver and downriver Aucas could live in peace. Dyuwi, the song leader for services in God's speaking house, composed a prayer hymn that expressed his desire: "Lord, You give us our land, and here, happily serving You, we will live."

In February, government officials came to Limoncocha for another meeting with representatives of the tribe. Gikita and young Kinta, nephew of Dyuwi, were there to represent the Aucas and ask for "lines carved on paper" that would recognize the tribe's rights to a tract of land in their traditional territory. The officials promised to have the documents drawn up.

Pilot Merrill Piper flew the two Aucas across downriver territory, and they spotted longhouses. When Merrill circled lower, they saw Aucas running into the houses. Gikita could hardly contain his excitement at this first sight of his hostile relatives since the last bloody battle of years past.

Gikita and Dyuwi were eager to get going. Again Rachel cautioned them to keep praying for God to send someone out from the downriver group who could serve as an intermediary.

Three months later, a radio message came that a wounded Auca girl was in a remote jungle settlement. Could Rachel come to see her?

Rachel found the girl, who looked about thirteen, burning up with fever in a settler's house. Her big balsa earplugs and bangs unmistakably marked her as an Auca.

The frightened girl was sullen and unresponsive until Rachel spoke in Auca and identified herself as Nimu. Nimu was the name of the girl's aunt, who had been shot by outsiders. "Are you one of us?" she asked Rachel.

"Father God sent me to live with your people at Tiwaeno. I am like a sister to Dayuma. We live happily and at peace."

The girl's eyes widened. "Does Dayuma still live? I was told the outsiders shot and ate her many years ago. They shot me. Will they eat me now?"

"No one will eat you," Rachel assured. "We want you to come and live happily with us at Tiwaeno. Now tell me your name."

"I—I am Oncaye. My mother is Titada." The names of other relatives poured out in a torrent, among them four sisters whom Rachel knew were at Tiwaeno.

"They are living?" Oncaye said incredulously. "I was told they had been speared by Gikita when they fled upriver years ago."

After Oncaye fell into a deep sleep, Rachel obtained permission to take her to the government military hospital in Shell Mera for surgery to remove the bullets. Two of her Tiwaeno sisters, Gakamo and Dawa, were flown to be with her in the hospital.

While recuperating, Oncaye told them that among the downriver group, bitter warfare was raging over wife stealing. The group was split into hostile factions of Aucas who were angry at each other and at the foreigners who had been moving closer.

The downriver girl spilled out her bitter memories. Her father had been speared when she was an infant. A few months later, the warrior Niwa had been plunked into her mother's hammock. Five younger children came along rapidly, forcing Oncaye to seek comfort and companionship from her grandmother. Then her Aunt Nimu was shot while trying to flee to the foreigners. In irrational frustration, one of her brothers speared their grandmother.

She knew that her stepfather, Niwa, had many enemies. The ones who came to kill her father would spear her brothers and kill or capture her. She was determined to flee first. Years before, some of her relatives had fled upriver and had not been heard from since. Her family presumed they had been killed by Gikita's group.

In desperation, Oncaye made the choice that Dayuma had, to risk going to the foreigners rather than remain and be killed or kidnapped. Her brothers agreed to pole her across Father River (the Napo) in a makeshift raft. Landing safely on the far shore, they took her to the spot where they had buried Aunt Nimu in a hollow log. The body had been pulled from the log, mutilated, and left to rot. Suddenly foreigners appeared in a canoe. Oncaye's brothers turned on them with spears. The outsiders fired their guns. Her brothers leaped into the water and escaped to the Auca side. Oncaye was not fast enough. The fire from a smoking stick slammed into her body, and she fell in a crumpled heap. The foreigners took her to the house in the settlement, where Rachel had found her burning with fever.

When the doctors released her, Oncaye willingly went to Tiwaeno with Rachel and her sisters. There she met her two other sisters. Boika, the older one, explained some of the changes that had come from hearing "God's Carving." "We who love the Lord no longer bury unwanted babies alive," she said.

The Tiwaeno relatives plied Oncaye for more information. Did she know of any plans to attack them? Where was the evil Niwa, who had speared so many of Gikita's family? Uncle Gikita explained that he had been training the young upriver men for an attack on Niwa and his warriors when Dayuma returned from the outside. Now, since believing in God's Son, Jesus, this desire had gone away. Gikita wanted only to meet his old enemy in peace and give him good words from "God's Carving."

"Niwa is very sick and can no longer fight," Oncaye said. "He may already be dead."

Sadness crossed Gikita's face, then renewed determination. "We must get medicines to him soon. He must hear God's Carving before he dies."

The Christians at Tiwaeno saw Oncaye as the key to reaching their downriver relatives. In February 1965, Dyuwi, Tona, Oncaye, and Boika set out with the intention of finding their downriver relatives and persuading them to come to Tiwaeno. It was felt best that Uncle Gikita not go, for his presence might provoke an immediate attack.

Boika found the trail she had used in escaping upriver

several years before. Farther along, she became confused and admitted she was lost. Oncaye's injury flared up painfully. A falling tree injured Tona's knee. Tired and discouraged, the quartet straggled back to Tiwaeno.

"I'm going the next time," Gikita insisted. Three weeks later, the oldest man at Tiwaeno, Dyuwi, and Minkayi set out with the hope of contacting their long-estranged relatives. The men knew they might be killed, but it was the thought of giving their fellow Aucas the good news from "God's Carving" that drove them on—the same motivation that had brought the five missionaries into Auca territory. Nimu's brother (Nate), Gikari's husband (Jim), and their three friends had died so that they might hear the gospel and live in peace. Now these faithful Aucas were willing to die, if necessary, in the effort to give their downriver kindred the same message.

Despite the noble intentions of three of the five Palm Beach killers, this second attempt also ended in failure. This time it was high water, caused by torrential rains, that blocked the path of Auca missionaries.

While attempts to penetrate the unreached downriver Aucas were going on, Rachel completed the gospel of Mark in Auca. The precious manuscript was sent off to Mexico City for printing by the American Bible Society.

The first Auca gospels were shipped back to Quito in time for dedication on Easter Sunday, 1965. Don Johnson and his wife, Helen, put the books in their station wagon, picked up Philip and Steve Saint at the HCJB guest house, and drove to Shell Mera. The Wycliffe plane flew them from there to Tiwaeno.

Don had helped bury the five martyrs. Later, in writing of his visits nine years apart, he reflected: "Then, I was carrying a rifle for protection. Now, I was taking the Sword of the Spirit to the people for whom my dear friends gave their lives."

They landed as the sun was setting Saturday evening and opened the boxes on the airstrip. Joy and delight illuminated the faces of the Aucas as they grasped the first books in their language. Thanks to reading classes that Rachel had recently held, some could pick out phrases and sentences. As Don snapped pictures of the memorable scene, Rachel and Cathy Peeke, who was back, working on the Auca grammar for her doctoral dissertation, stood nearby, holding their own books, savoring the thrill of the occasion. Philip and Steve, ages eleven and fourteen respectively, looked on, remembering that their father and his four friends had died to make this moment possible.

The next morning, they gathered in God's speaking-house for the Easter dedication. The Aucas sang a hymn chant, then Rachel led everyone in a unison recital of memorized Scripture. Dyuwi launched the children into a spirited, animated songfest. Rachel explained how the books had been translated and printed and had a number of Aucas read verses. Now it was time for the message, and Don spoke, as a layman, on the meaning of the resurrection, with Rachel interpreting. Kimo concluded with the unforgettable dedicatory prayer.

"Father God, You are alive," he solemnly said. "This is Your day, and all of us are here to worship You. You are all-powerful and all-knowing. Father God, Your Carving they brought, enough for everybody. We happily take it and, having taken it, all of us read, and, seeing it, we say, 'This is truth.' And if we didn't have it and were empty-handed as before, how would we be living? We would jus be existing like animals. Father God, while we live in this land, Your Carving always we will obey."

The Johnsons and Philip returned to Quito. Steve planned to remain with his Aunt Rachel until his mother came out for her vacation in June. His older sister, Kathy, would then be home from Hampden Dubose Academy in Florida and would accompany Philip and their mother back to Tiwaeno.

Steve had been coming on visits to Tiwaeno since he was eleven and felt right at home. The first time he stepped off the plane as a beanpole-skinny white kid with blond hair and black-rimmed glasses, an Auca baby screamed and older children scurried off. After a few days, the novelty of his presence wore off, and the young boys took him to hunt monkeys. He tried hard but never learned to shoot a blowgun with the accuracy of an Auca.

During a number of vacations, his sister, Kathy, now a beautiful young woman of sixteen and a junior in high school, had provided companionship and assistance to her Aunt Rachel. The very first time, she had taken over the cooking and told her aunt, "Go on with your translation work. Don't worry about interpreting. I'll learn how to talk Auca myself."

She got along beautifully until one day when she had to call for assistance. "Aunt Rachel, Oba is trying very hard to tell me something. What is she saying?"

Rachel listened closely and replied, "She's saying that her father was speared."

"Was her daddy speared, too?" Kathy said with a gasp.

"Yes, Kathy dear, almost everybody here except the children of the seven men will tell you the same thing: 'My father was speared. My mother was speared.' "

"They can understand how I felt when my daddy was killed?"

"Yes."

From that day on, Kathy felt a special identification—
almost a kinship—with the Aucas. Now, awaiting the
end of her school year in Florida, she was anticipating
seeing them again.

Years before, she had trusted Christ as her Savior but
had never been baptized. Recently she had heard that
Beth Youderian had been baptized by the Jivaros, "Because they are my people." *Why can't I be baptized by my
people, the Aucas?* she thought.

She wrote her mother:

The Aucas have been very special people to me
since Daddy was killed, especially Kimo and
Dawa. When I was staying with Aunt Rachel they
would come over to her house and we would sit
and talk. I remember asking them, "What if right
now the downriver group should come and try to
spear us, what would you do?" Dawa would say,
"There's nothing we could do but run and risk it,
or stay and pray." And Kimo would agree with
her. Their simple, childlike faith really impressed
me.

Mother, I trust the Aucas' Christianity. It isn't
just something to do. It costs them something. I
doubt a lot of the Christianity I see. I even doubt a
lot of my own Christianity as being cultural. That's
why I would like to be baptized by the Aucas.

Marj saw no reason why she shouldn't be and talked
to Rachel on the radio. "It's fine with me," Rachel said.
"Let me talk to some of the Aucas and your brother
Steve."

In a few minutes, Steve came on the radio to say it
would be OK. Oncaye, the girl from downriver, and a
teenage boy, Iniwa, were ready for baptism also. "I'd

like to be baptized, too," Steve said, "here among the people Dad wanted to reach."

At Dayuma's invitation, Marj planned a trip to Palm Beach. Dayuma had some crops growing there, and she thought Marj might like to see the grave of Nate and his friends. It was Don Johnson who suggested, "If you're going to the beach anyway, why not have your children baptized there?"

The entourage left Tiwaeno on June 25 for the two-day trail and canoe trip to the site so hallowed in their memories. They found the beach halfway underwater, as the Aucas had said it was. Obviously, no plane could land there now. And Kimo pointed out something else that seemed more than circumstantial. An ancestral Auca trail directly crossed the beach. "If they hadn't landed here," he said, "our hunters would never have heard the chopping."

They came across the spot where the five missionaries had built their ground shelter, estimated where the wrecked plane had stood before flood waters washed it downstream, and located the stump of the tree that had supported the tree house. Pushing ahead of the rest, Kimo and Dyuwi led the way through dense undergrowth to the slight mound that marked the grave. Tears flowed freely as Americans and Aucas gathered around the sacred spot and sang the martyrs' favorite hymn, "We Rest on Thee." When they looked up from prayer, Rachel noticed five red jungle flowers standing straight and tall. To her they symbolized the five men who had given their lives.

They gathered along the water's edge for the baptismal service. Dayuma quoted from the newly translated gospel of Mark. Dyuwi sang the Auca equivalent of "Jesus Loves Me." Then Kimo and the four teenagers waded into the water. Kimo talked to each of the four, emphasizing that by their public baptism, they were declaring their unconditional love for God and their commitment to walk worthily before Him. Then the Auca entered each into the water, baptizing them in the name of the Father and His Son and the Holy Spirit. Remembering the sad event of 1956, Kimo prayed, "Father God, You know we sinned here. We were ignorant. We did not know our brothers had come to tell us about You. Now You have put our sins in the deepest water, and happily we serve You and know that we will see those we killed again. Father God, these young brothers and sisters have entered into the water. Help them to live happily, as we do. Help them to be true to You and Your Carving."

Marj and Philip returned to Quito. Kathy and Steve remained in Tiwaeno with their Auca friends a few weeks longer, then went to Quito for the rest of their vacation. This left Rachel with Cathy Peeke, who was finishing research for her doctoral dissertation.

Dr. and Mrs. Edman came in November 1965 to hold a Bible conference for the Aucas. Prexy's interest in the group had never ceased.

The conference climaxed with the first Auca communion. After Dr. Edman taught them from Scripture, Kimo took the bowl of boiled manioc, offered prayer, and served the "bread." Dyuwi then served a banana drink, the "wine," from a gourd.

The commissioning of the first native Auca missionaries followed. Dr. Edman read from Acts 13 about the dispatch of Paul and Barnabas by the believers at Antioch to be missionaries to the Gentile world. As he reported in a later press release, "Dyuwi and Tona, who felt called to go to their wild and wicked downriver enemies, and Oncaye, the little Auca girl rescued from those same enemies, came and knelt." Then the commitment was given in three languages: Mr. Taber, a visiting businessman, in English; Dr. Edman, in Spanish; and Kimo, in Auca. Dr. Edman prayed that the Holy Spirit would send them forth as truly as He had sent Barnabas and Paul from the early church.

Reaching the downriver people was now even more critical. The oil workers were advancing deeper into Auca territory. Within ten years, miles of pipeline would carry the black gold from the jungle across the Andes to the port of Esmeraldas on the Pacific. Along the newly built road that ran near the pipeline would come more homesteaders.

The oil companies, the government, and SIL kept their lines of communication open. Pilots for both SIL and the oil companies kept a sharp eye out for Auca dwellings. Often when a sighting was made, a SIL pilot would go back the next day and see no sign of life. The elusive, wild Aucas seemed to stay on the run.

In February 1966, pilot Don Smith spotted a cluster of houses downriver, several miles from previously sighted huts. He picked up Dayuma, Dyuwi, and Oncaye, for a closer look. When he swooped low, Oncaye saw her mother and another woman running to hide. But a big, muscular man stood defiantly in the clearing and raised spears in threatening gestures.

Dyuwi, Tona, Oncaye, and Boika set out again from Tiwaeno. They carried a small supply of food and medicine and a radio for keeping in contact with Tiwaeno and Limoncocha. Don Smith was to fly over them every day and guide them to the new houses.

Several days downriver, they came upon footprints that Oncaye said belonged to members of her family. A little way on, they noticed dark stains on the ground beside one pair of prints: blood. Oncaye and Boika followed these prints up a side trail.

The sun fell, and the darkness that comes quickly near the equator was almost on them when they were stopped by a nauseating stench and the flapping of wings. Peering through the gathering gloom, they made out a small hut in a clearing filled with buzzards. Oncaye crept closer and saw spears protruding from a body. "Mother!" she screamed. The two sisters turned and ran back to warn Dyuwi and Tona.

They ran a long way through the darkness, not stopping to rest and build a fire until they felt safe. Dyuwi and Tona fell asleep almost instantly, while Boika and Oncaye stayed up to chew chonta-palm nuts, preparing food for the next day. A few moments later, both girls sensed spies in the bush. Passing a telling look, they began talking for the benefit of the unseen listeners.

Oncaye: "I feel very sad. We came this long way to find my mother and brothers and bring them to live happily at Tiwaeno and learn about Father God and His Carving. Now we find Mother is dead."

Boika: "Oh, I am unhappy, too. I only hope they do not go to Father River, where others wait to shoot them. I wish they would move near us, where we could teach them about Father God."

They heard a telltale whistle, the signal among Auca eavesdroppers to attack. "So! You plan to spear me, too!" Oncaye called into the forest. "Well, go ahead and try it. You can't hurt me. You will just kill my body. My soul will go to be with Father God!"

Dyuwi and Tona were now awake. Grabbing their supplies, the four ran toward Tiwaeno. As they fled through the forest, Oncaye realized the enemy would be following their footprints. "Father God, make it rain," she prayed. "Hurry!" The clouds opened up and unloaded a downpour that obliterated their tracks.

Ten eventful years had now passed since Palm Beach. The decade had brought the conversion of the killers, the birth of the Auca church, the translation of one gospel into Auca, and the first attempts at Auca missionary outreach.

HCJB marked the anniversary by in-person reports from Rachel Saint. Uncle Cam Townsend reminded Eucadorian officials of the event, and the government issued commemorative postage stamps for each of the five slain missionaries. No South American country had ever honored evangelical missionaries in this way. In Shell Mera, the Nate Saint Memorial School for missionary children was opened.

Dr. Edman wrote articles about "the first Auca communion." Billy Graham's *Decision*, the Christian magazine with the widest circulation, published a dramatic photo-and-text story on the five killers. The Graham organization also distributed over a hundred thousand copies of a booklet by Rachel, *Ten Years After the Massacre*.

Surprisingly, many readers learned for the first time that Betty Elliot had been gone from the Aucas for almost four years, though they were not given all her reasons for leaving. Many also discovered for the first time that Rachel was the sister of Nate Saint, not his wife.

Some publications provided brief updates on the five widows, showing they had not been forgotten. Marj was still in service with HCJB. Barbara was now managing the Gospel Missionary Union's guest house in Quito. Marilou had decided not to return after her stay in New Jersey and had moved to Seattle, Washington, where several of Ed's relatives lived. Her brother-in-law, Bill Erickson, helped her get a job in the administrative office of a suburban hospital. Her oldest son,

Steve, was now a teenager. Betty was busy being a mother to eleven-year-old Valerie and keeping up with writing and speaking opportunities. Olive, still the only one to have remarried, had a daughter, Beverly, to complement her son.

The four single widows had all been asked if they planned to remarry. Betty had told Marilou she did not think she would. Marilou had had several suitors, but she felt none was prepared to be a father to three growing boys. Beth Youderian had encouraged her mother to remarry, but Barbara remained single by choice.

To questioners, Marj had always answered, "Someday, perhaps, but after I get my children raised. I wouldn't marry anyone who didn't love my children as I do."

Steve and Kathy, both away in school, had recently been talking about how they would care for their mother in her old age. "We don't want you to think you ever need to get married," they wrote her. "We'll always take good care of you."

Back came a letter saying that Abe Van Der Puy had proposed. Abe's beloved Delores had succumed to cancer the year before, leaving him with three children: Joe, Mark, and Lois, ages fourteen, sixteen, and twenty, respectively. The Van Der Puy and Saint kids had been next-door neighbors, schoolmates at the Alliance Academy, and close friends. Everyone who knew them said that the marriage would be like bringing six brothers and sisters together under the same roof.

The Saint kids were overjoyed. "If it's Uncle Abe," Steve wrote, "that's different. When is the date?" Abe had always been one of their favorite missionary "uncles," the one who had taken them fishing with his boys and looked out for them since their father's death. Before going to Florida, Kathy had told Marj, "If anything happens to you, we'd like Uncle Abe to be responsible for the three of us. He is the nicest older man we know."

So, with the happy approval of all concerned, Marj and Abe were married on August 25, 1966, before 800 guests on the HCJB compound. Dr. Reuben Larson, cofounder of the World Missionary Radio Fellowship, owners of HCJB, and Senor Enrique Romero officiated, giving the service in both Spanish and English. All the children were involved. Kathy was her mother's maid of honor. Lois sang. Mark "stood up" for the groom. Steve, Phil, and Joe ushered.

When the wedding photos were developed, Marj sent a pictorial record to friends and relatives who could not attend. "We're having a delightful time together as a family," she wrote. "All eight of us desire that the Lord use our lives and our home for His honor." The letter was signed, "Happy as can be, Abe and Marj."

"I say to you, take God's Carving to all the
people in your lands. We will go home and take
God's message to our downriver enemies."
Kimo

Missionaries Abroad and at Home 9

The summer of the baptisms on Palm Beach, Uncle
Cam brought Chief Tariri to the New York
World's Fair, where Wycliffe had a pavilion. Tariri was
the hit of the New York media, appearing on the NBC
"Today" show, riding in the gondola of the Goodyear
blimp, and speaking for Peru Day at the Fair.

Uncle Cam felt that people who visited his organization's pavilion at the New York World's Fair would be
blessed to hear the old former headshrinker tell of how
God had taken the hatred out of his heart, filling it with
love instead. It would show them the value of giving
even headhunters in the jungle the Word of God in
their own tongues.

When Billy Graham and others began planning a
World Congress of Evangelism in Berlin, they immediately thought of the Aucas. Why not have Uncle
Cam bring one or two of the converted killers as delegates to the congress, which would be attended by
church leaders from all nations? Uncle Cam declined
himself but encouraged George Cowan, president of
Wycliffe, to go in his place.

Rachel reluctantly agreed to escort two Aucas and be
their interpreter if their appearance would heighten

awareness of the Bible-translation cause. Some Wycliffe people worried that the intense public exposure might hurt the Aucas and create problems when they returned to the tribe. As one said, "How are you gonna keep 'em in the jungle after they've seen Berlin?" Betty Elliot spoke her piece (she was opposed) to a reporter for the *Boston Globe*, but the newspaper did not print her opinions.

Kimo and Komi were chosen to go. Before they stepped on the plane, Rachel told them, "When I'm in your country, where you know your way around, I listen to you. When you're in my country, you listen to me."

They were the first Auca men to fly out of the jungle. When they landed in Quito, their heads were swiveling. As they stepped out of the plane, a truck rolled in front of them. "Look, there's an airplane walking!" exclaimed the amazed Kimo, who had never seen such a vehicle.

Rachel took them first to her home in suburban Philadelphia for much-needed dental work and outfitting in suits, overcoats, dress shoes, hats, and scarfs to protect their throats in the cold climate. They met Rachel's brothers and her mother. The Indians had never seen a person as old as Mrs. Saint.

Kimo developed a fever on the flight across the Atlantic; then he got better and Komi became ill. Rachel stayed with Komi while George Cowan took Kimo to the sessions of the congress in the ultramodern Kongress Halle, near the Berlin Wall. The 1,111 delegates represented churches from over 100 countries. Many wore their native regalia. Kimo stared and marveled at the size of "God's believing family," as the Aucas had come to call the community of believers.

Komi's health improved, and Rachel took both Aucas

to the park. The only wildlife they saw was a little mouse. They kept looking for monkeys in trees and finally decided why there were none. "The trees are too short and too far apart for monkeys to jump from one treetop to another," Kimo explained. They kept looking for the sun in the sky that stayed overcast and drizzly all week. It was the only way they knew how to tell time.

The presence of the two Aucas at the congress was well-known. Few delegates had not heard of the Palm Beach massacre, although some did not know what had happened since. The color of the Aucas' skin did not stand out, for there were delegates from many nations at the congress. It was the entourage of reporters and cameramen that always signaled their whereabouts. German television crews trailed them; CBS shot footage for showing in the United States. *Life* photographers took pictures for a "Ten Years After Palm Beach" story.

Rachel was an attraction herself. Some delegates had read *The Dayuma Story*, which had been translated into three European languages. A Finnish woman credited the book with "getting me into Christian work."

Before leaving Quito, Rachel had picked up eight copies of a Russian book Jack Shalanko had written about the sacrifice of the five fellows. She looked for Russian delegates, but none had been allowed to come. Then a Hungarian preacher came up to meet the Aucas. Rachel pulled out a book and showed him Kimo's and Komi's pictures and the Russian text. "Where can I buy a copy?" he asked eagerly. "You may have this one," Rachel offered. He grabbed the book and disappeared into the crowd.

The next morning, Peter Dyneka, a Russian emigrant to Canada and head of the Slavic Gospel Mission, and several more delegates from the satellite countries met Rachel and the Aucas at the door of the Kongress Halle.

They had heard about the Russian book from the Hungarian and wondered if Rachel had more. She gave them her remaining copies. Years later she heard that a woman had copied the book by hand, a chapter at a time, and mailed it into Russia as letters.

Rachel also brought a small packet of the commemorative Ecuadorian stamps bearing pictures of the five martyrs. She gave a set to a man from Asia. Within minutes she was besieged by other Asians. "Do you have any more of those stamps, Miss Saint?" a Korean pleaded. "All we ever heard was that they were killed."

The Aucas' time on the program came Saturday night, October 29. George Cowan interviewed them, with Rachel interpreting. Kimo did most of the talking. Some of the recorded conversation went like this:

Q. *What did your forefathers believe about God?*
A. They spoke just a little about God and then went off the trail. They did not teach us the truth. They lived in great fear.
Q. *Why did they live in such fear?*
A. They were afraid of their own relatives who lived being very mad. So they speared the foreigners, too.
Q. *Who first told you about the Lord Jesus Christ?*
A. Dayuma came and said to me, "Why don't you understand? Up in heaven the living God is, and you must make it your purpose really to believe in Him."
Q. *How has Jesus changed your life?*
A. I don't live the same way I did before. I don't live sinning now. Now I live speaking to God.
Q. *Do you have a message for the believers here, who come from all over the world?*
A. I say to you, take God's Carving to all the peo-

ple in your lands. We will go home and take God's message to our downriver enemies. We will say to them, "Believing in God and His Son Jesus, we live well. We have stopped spearing and choking babies. We live happily with our families." This we will say and invite them to believe in God and live in peace with us.

When Rachel finished interpreting the Auca's remarks, the hall rang with amens and shouts of praise. In the audience were Abe and Marj Van Der Puy, who were attending the congress on a belated honeymoon.

Cliff Barrows, song leader for the congress, jumped up and asked Rachel if the two Aucas would sing for the delegates. At her request, the uninhibited pair broke into a repetitive chant, with Barrows trying to hum along with them.

"Praise the Lord!" Barrows exclaimed. "Praise the Lord!" Then he asked everyone to stand and join in a closing hymn of a more familiar pattern. While they were singing, an African delegate ran from the crowd and jumped up on the platform to hug each of the Aucas. Kimo looked bewildered. Komi smiled as if he enjoyed it. The impulsive act just about broke up the meeting. George Cowan overheard one delegate say, "The African did just what we all wanted to do."

The congress climaxed on Reformation Sunday with a public parade from Wittenberg Plaza to the Kaiser Wilhelm Memorial Church, where Billy Graham preached to an overflow crowd. Kimo and Komi, wearing their uncomfortable suits and overcoats and feather headpieces, marched up front beside Tom Klaus, an American Iroquois Indian, and just behind evangelist Graham and the German leaders of the procession.

From Berlin, the Aucas traveled by train to Switzerland. When the train nosed into the first tunnel, they moaned in fright. Rachel had a hard time reassuring them they would see day again.

As they neared the border, a customs inspector came up to them. "Do you speak English, Italian, Spanish? Are you Eskimos?" At Rachel's nod they gave their first names and sat there as if everyone ought to know them.

From Switzerland, they went to London for appearances before Christian groups. They faced more crowds, more questions, more cameras, and media interviews.

When they returned home after six weeks abroad, Kimo lay in his hammock a long time, thinking of all he had seen. It was not the freeways, the tall buildings, the huge airplanes, or the "caves" (hotels) in which they had stayed that most impressed him. It was the myriads of people—more people than he had ever imagined. On the following Sunday, he tried to help kinspeople comprehend the numbers. "Look at all the trees around us," he said. "Look as far as you can see. Beyond the hills and mountains are more trees. Think of all the leaves on all the trees. That's how many foreigners there are."

While Kimo and Komi were still getting over the culture shock of their trip abroad, news came that wild Aucas had killed another Quichua, on the Napo. "We must find my people and give them God's Carving before they kill again," the determined Oncaye said. But Dyuwi was sick and Tona, the best reader in Tiwaeno, was needed for teaching. Dawa agreed to accompany Oncaye on the fourth attempt. Her husband, Kimo, and Minkayi would go partway and wait.

The two young women found only deserted and burned houses. They left gifts of bright-colored cloth and turned back to meet the two men and return to Tiwaeno.

Pilots located a new group of houses on a small river. This time a Tiwaeno missionary party ended up on the wrong river, but they discovered footprints and signs indicating a large party of men had come out with spears to meet them. Five trips had been made without success. With the oil companies pressing closer, time was quickly running out. If the downriver Aucas were not reached and pacified soon, perhaps within a few months, it might be too late.

The Christians at Tiwaeno prayed. Wycliffe personnel prayed. Thousands of Christians who received newsletters from Wycliffe members whom they supported prayed.

A pilot located more houses. He took Oncaye back over the area and flew low. They saw people on the ground. A small boy ran across the clearing as if he were trying to keep up with the plane. "Awa!" Oncaye shouted. "That's my little brother, Awa!" She called down to the people who had vanished into the house. "I am Oncaye! I am Oncaye! I come in peace!" There was no way her family could respond.

Around Christmas 1967, the ingenious Don Smith came up with the idea of dropping a basket with a hidden transmitter, using Nate Saint's spiral drop. On the first try the basket hit the ground too hard. He then wrapped an antenna around a plastic bowl and stuck a tin container that shielded a transmitter inside the bowl. On a flight over the houses with Oncaye, he dropped the bowl by parachute. The chute landed in a tree, but they heard the voices of men climbing to get it. A moment later, the voices stopped. The Aucas had ripped the transmitter away from its aerial connection.

Don Johnson thought a transmitter might be hidden in the false bottom of a gift-laden basket and the antenna woven into the basket. They parachuted this into the clearing where Oncaye had seen her brother. A naked Auca stood looking at the basket in wonder. "Who are you?" Oncaye called to him.

"I am Dabu!"

Oncaye recognized the voice. "No, you're my brother Tyaento, and I am your sister Oncaye. We have come in peace. Walk toward Moipa's field, and we will meet you on the trail. We will leave from upriver, early in the morning."

"Bring me a foreigner's ax," he bargained. "I will come."

Quivering with excitement, Oncaye, Dawa, Kimo, and Dyuwi set out from Tiwaeno with a radio, food, and medicines. Four days later, February 15, 1968, Don Smith, Rachel, and Dayuma followed in the plane. They found the houses deserted, but Dayuma spotted smoke rising through clouds ahead.

Don flew just above trees near where the smoke was coming from. "Tyaento," Dayuma called through the loudspeaker on the wing, "if you are there, make more smoke." Smoke mushroomed from the ground.

Don flew on and located Oncaye and Dawa, coming from Tiwaeno. Dayuma gave them the good news. The women began sprinting. Dawa, weakened by a recent illness, had to stop and rest. The downriver girl saw footprints, heard voices, then saw her mother, Titada, whom she had believed to be dead. "Mother! Mother! I am your daughter, Oncaye." Others were running away. The woman turned her head in bewilderment.

"Mother! I am Oncaye."

Titada had not seen her daughter in four years, and Oncaye was wearing clothes. But she recognized her. It *was* Oncaye. "I thought you were killed by the outsiders," she said in a trembling voice.

"And I thought *you* had been speared and eaten by the buzzards, mother!"

Dawa came up, huffing and puffing. While Oncaye and Titada talked, she looked around and glimpsed a hammock swaying slightly between trees. The woman in the hammock was Wina, Tyaento's young wife. Bitten by a poisonous snake, Oncaye's sister-in-law had been left to die.

"We will give you medicine and pray that Father God will save your life," Dawa assured her.

One by one the others emerged from the forest. There was Wina's two small children and Awa and Tyaento.

With Tyaento's permission, Dawa, who had been trained by Rachel, administered serum to Wina. This brought the swelling down, but they needed to get her to Tiwaeno for more treatment. Kimo and Dyuwi, who had stayed back, came and met their long-lost, down-river relatives. Kimo volunteered to carry Wina back over the long trail.

Oncaye plied her mother with queries about other members of her family. Titada told her that her step-father, Niwa, the enemy for whom Gikita had been so concerned, was dead from the smoking sticks of outsiders. As he lay dying, he begged his brother and sons never to spear again. Ignoring his plea, his brother and others sought to kill his wives so that they might join him in the grave. One of the wives killed was Bogani, who happened to be Dyuwi's half-sister. It was her decaying body that Oncaye had mistaken for Titada's.

In pursuing Titada and the children, the killers had run upon a herd of wild hogs and expended their fury in killing the animals. When they reached the runaways, they simply told them to go back home.

Oncaye shuddered, thinking how close her mother had come to being killed.

The four upriver Auca Christians and Oncaye's family hurried along through the forest, well aware that Niwa's brother and sons might be pursuing them. After a seven-day trek, they reached Tiwaeno, and Oncaye introduced her family to Rachel. The next Sunday, Oncaye had her whole family in God's speaking-house to hear Kimo preach. The first to believe was Tewae, one of Oncaye's brothers. He married the daughter of Dabu, marking the first marriage between members of the two groups in over twelve years.

Twelve years had elapsed since Palm Beach, almost ten years had passed since the entry. From a population of fifty-six (which included sixteen refugees from downriver), the Tiwaeno group was now up to one hundred four. Eleven newcomers could easily be fed and housed in a community of this size.

But the task was not complete, for Oncaye's family said many more people were roaming the downriver forests. In June 1968, Titada and Oncaye left on another journey downriver. Rachel and Tyaento flew ahead of them and circled the major clearing. Tyaento called through the loudspeaker to a large crowd and invited them to meet Titada and Oncaye on the trail.

At the appointed time, Oncaye radioed that the first ones from the larger group had arrived, starving and burning with fever from flu. Weaker ones were still on the trail.

Dyuwi led a rescue party from Tiwaeno, with food and medicines. They met Oncaye and her mother leading their old downriver enemies along a muddy trail. Weakened by hunger and sickness, the pitiful stragglers could hardly walk.

The Tiwaeno Aucas fed their helpless enemies and

administered medicines. After a time of rest, they started on for Tiwaeno. Along the way, a downriver man collapsed and moaned that he could go no farther. "Climb on my back," Dyuwi invited. Soon another fell, then another. Each was taken up and carried by a Tiwaeno Christian.

Rachel did not know how many would be coming. As they staggered in by small groups, she was too busy to keep count. Finally the last one arrived. As she determined later, ninety-three new ones from downriver, plus the eleven members of Oncaye's family who had come earlier, made one hundred four. This exactly doubled the population of Tiwaeno.

It was not the most propitious time to have company. The weather was cool and rainy, the ground soggy, and the water too high to catch fish. The Christians couldn't get to their fields or into the forest to hunt game. Rachel had a few boxes of CARE food that had been flown in to supplement the local supply of manioc and monkey meat, but the newcomers would not eat this unfamiliar fare. Another difficulty was housing. There was hardly enough room for so many.

Something else worried Rachel. The newcomers were raw pagans, hardened killers, who in the past had vowed to wipe out their upriver cousins. Now they were too weak to help themselves, but what would happen when the flu subsided and they became stronger?

There was little time to think of that, however. Tiwaeno was a field hospital without doctor or nurse. The sick had to be cared for, the hungry fed. Rachel did not have to tell the Tiwaeno Christians what to do. They knew from years of Dayuma's teachings and instructions from Scripture. They took their old enemies into their huts, shared their food, and tenderly watched over the sick ones day and night. As for Rachel, she and

Dawa went from house to house, checking temperatures, dispensing medicine, comforting babies, and giving support to the ministering Christians. Dayuma was limited in what she could do, for she and Komi now had two small children to look after, the younger of whom was blind from birth.

Rachel had kept Limoncocha informed of the crisis. Just as food supplies were running dangerously low, a SIL plane flew over and parachuted more CARE packages and medicines, along with manioc and bananas. The jungle foodstuffs had been brought to Limoncocha by Christian Quichuas who had heard about the shortage in Tiwaeno. The pilot did not land, because Rachel feared that would not be safe.

The men of Tiwaeno were not unaware of the potential for trouble. Lest anyone misunderstand, they went around announcing the Christian lifestyle of Tiwaeno: "Here we do not kill fellowmen, Aucas or outsiders. Here a man does not take his wife's sisters or anyone else who is not his spouse. Here we do not kill our babies or throw them in the river. Here we obey God's Carving and believe in His Son, Jesus, who died for us. Here we live happily and in peace. Here we want you to believe in God and live in peace with us."

Sure enough, when the flu victims began recovering their strength, some of the newcomers began causing problems. One of the men wanted Dyuwi's young daughter as a second wife. Dyuwi refused. "You may spear me," he said, "but God's Carving says we are to have only one wife." The man stalked away.

Uncle Gikita's house guest, who already had two wives, wanted to sleep with Gikita's spouse, and the visitor's sons wanted privileges with Gikita's married daughter. When Gikita said no, the man and his sons began whittling spears. Rather than engage in a fight,

Gikita took his family to the Curaray River and built a new home.

The key person in policing the troublemakers turned out to be Dawa. She was a half-sister to the deceased Niwa, who had been the leader of the downriver group, and by the kinship pattern, she was "grandmother" to numerous children and in-laws, including most of the downriver men. During the daytime she went around preaching against the old murderous and adulterous ways. At night she made hammock checks to see that no one was roaming around with hatred in his heart. When she found an empty hammock, she located the occupant and brought him back. No one else among the Christians dared be out at night.

The Tiwaeno men enlarged God's speaking-house to make room for the newcomers. Dyuwi called on the congregation to pray that other long-lost relatives might be found. Kimo was not so enthusiastic. His wife, Dawa, was up day and night, keeping her kinspeople in line. Oncaye's brother, Tyaento, was threatening to kill his little daughter if his sick son died. "I'm not bringing anyone else who wants to kill babies," Kimo declared.

Rachel quietly reminded him that Tyaento's heart had not been changed. Kimo thought about that a while. He also remembered what he had said in Berlin and a verse that Rachel had recently translated that said, "Ye shall be witnesses unto me both in Jerusalem, and in all Judaea, and in Samaria, and unto the uttermost part of the earth" (Acts 1:8, KJV). As a believer, he seemed to have no other choice. "Following God, I will go after others," he told Rachel.

The weather cleared up. The women were able to get into their fields to work and the men into the forest to hunt. Some of the downriver families moved out a few miles, cleared land, and built their own houses. A number declared themselves believers and followers of the new way. The pressure eased, though Tiwaeno would never again be the same.

It had been six years since the Aucas asked the Ecuadorian government for a guarantee of land rights. In January 1969, the government completed the paper-work granting them a protectorate covering about 40,000 acres, around one-tenth of the Aucas' traditional territory. This did not include mineral rights, for in Ecuador as in many other countries, the subsoil wealth is set aside for the nation.

The oil companies were mapping every square mile of the old territory. The jungle was alive with planes and helicopters, and the geologists were being proved right. There were rich oil reserves under the ground on which for centuries Aucas had hunted, fished, and farmed.

Some of the downriver families had gone back to their old haunts. There were other wild Aucas still roaming around the rest of the old territory—at least a hundred more, it was estimated. Sporadic attacks on oil crews and settlers continued.

Rachel and Dayuma wanted all the wild Aucas brought into the protectorate to keep them from killing outsiders and for their own protection. They proposed that they come a family or two at a time to avoid a sudden influx like the last one. Some Wycliffe members doubted the wisdom of this plan. The Aucas, they suggested, were a long way from even a self-supporting agricultural economy. In an area half the size of Rhode Island, they predicted that the game and fish supply would soon be depleted.

Dayuma sent word to all the downriver Aucas who had left in recent months that they should return to Tiwaeno. All came except the family of Downriver Dabu. One of old Niwa's sons, he did not like Christian

morals and said so. Other messengers went to make a
second plea and were told that he had been bitten by a
snake and was close to death, hidden in a deep ravine
with his family. On foot, Oncaye and other Christians
from Tiwaeno took medication and food to him. After
they returned, an oil helicopter dropped Cathy Peeke
into the ravine. She rounded up the scared group and
persuaded them to return to Tiwaeno, where they could
be cared for.

Two of Dawa's brothers, Baiwa and Babae, had never
come up from downriver. Titada, Oncaye's mother, recalled that many years before, they had fled with their
families into the southern forest. She thought they
might still be alive.

A pilot located some houses beside a small stream in
that area and flew Rachel and Titada over for a look.
"Baiwa! Baiwa!" Titada shouted to naked figures on the
ground. A man she believed to be Baiwa waved back.

When they flew over again, ten bronzed men yelled
and tossed spears at the plane. On a succeeding flight,
Kimo talked through a loudspeaker and was told,
through a basket transmitter on the ground, that Oma-
toki, a sister Dayuma had thought dead, was alive and
married to Baiwa. Then a man ran out, brandishing a
spear and screaming, "Foreigners! Foreigners! I'll separate their souls from their skins!" Dawa, who was also
in the plane, exclaimed, "That's my brother Babae! I
know his voice."

On one of these flights, the searchers spotted another
bunch of wild Aucas on a high ridge about fifteen minutes by plane from Baiwa's clearing. Rachel dropped
an electronic basket in the clearing and turned on her
recorder. These Aucas refused to go near the transmitter.

That evening as she listened to the tape, not really

expecting to hear anything, a faint voice identified himself as "Tona." She thought that he and the Tona in the Tiwaeno might be named for the same grandfather—an Auca custom.

Tiwaeno Tona was flown over the clearing on the ridge. "I, Tona, son of Coba, come to you. Wave if you hear me." A flock of arms shot up.

Tona saw one man whom he thought was his older brother, Wepe. He called him by name, and he waved back. The pilot kept circling while Tona talked, asking them to stop spearing, telling them of the new faith, promising to come to them.

On another flight, one of the Aucas in the ridge clearing pointed south and said he was going to visit Nampawae. Tona almost jumped out of his seat. Nampawae was the name of a brother-in-law. Did his sister, Omade, still live?

By spring 1969, the oil crews had pushed to within twenty-five miles of Baiwa's clearing. Rachel feared more killings if something wasn't done. She flew out to meet with Don Johnson and some oil executives.

"If you go in there, you'll lose some men," Rachel warned.

When the oil men expressed doubt, Rachel played a tape of Auca screams and yells. "I recorded those from a transmitter dropped in Baiwa's clearing," she noted. "They're throwing spears at the plane."

"What are they yelling?" one of the oil men asked.

" 'You foreign devils, we'll separate your souls from your skins!' They're killers, I tell you. They'll spear anybody who goes near them."

The oil men were impressed. "We don't want anybody killed. We'll wait a little longer."

In July 1969, just before Neil Armstrong walked on the moon, Kimo and Dawa walked into Baiwa's clearing

and talked with her brothers. Dawa told them that foreigners were coming with big pipes to suck liquid fire
from the earth. She begged them to come to Tiwaeno,
where other relatives were believing in God and living
well.

Back in Tiwaeno, Rachel's pastor brother, Ben Saint,
had come to hold a Bible conference and baptize several
new believers. Sammy Padilla, Dayuma's son, was
there, spending his school vacation with his mother.
When Kimo radioed that Baiwa's group was coming
out, Dayuma, Sammy, and most of the Christian men in
Tiwaeno set out to meet them. Rachel became concerned for Ben's safety among the unconverted downriver killers left in the village. She called for a plane.

When Ben landed in Limoncocha, he was met with
the news that their mother was critically ill. He radioed
Rachel the sad report.

Rachael was alone again in the tribe. She had not
gone home when her father died six years before. She
yearned to see her mother one more time. But Baiwa's
wild group was coming, and she felt she should be in
Tiwaeno when they arrived. Her commitment and calling had to come before her family. "Go on home to
mother," she told Ben. "Tell them that I love them and
will be praying. Ask them to pray for me. Nobody
knows what will happen when Baiwa and his people
get here."

It was August before the contact party arrived back in
Tiwaeno, bringing fifty-six more wild Aucas with them.
Baiwa wore the parachute used to drop the electronic
transmitter. Another man had the cloth that lined the
basket wrapped around his body. More residents of
Tiwaeno lined the riverbank to welcome them. Others
fled into the jungle, fearful of treachery from the notorious Baiwa.

Baiwa showed no hostility, not even when he met Rachel. "I heard Kimo's message from the plane," he said. "I did not kill the outsiders who came to suck the liquid fire from the earth. I only stole their manioc." They later learned that this was a lie.

Again, Dawa took the lead in teaching the newcomers. For two weeks she hardly slept or ate. Then, on August 30 she was called to help Amoncawa, a young man from a downriver family that had moved near the Curaray. He died before she got there, partially paralyzed and drooling at the mouth, the relatives said.

Katherine Saint died September 2. The day Rachel received the death message, Amoncawa's mother was brought to Tiwaeno, suffering the symptoms of her son's fatal illness. Rachel and Dawa were unable to save her.

Rachel radioed Lois Pederson, the Wycliffe nurse at Limoncocha, and gave her the symptoms.

"I can't be sure," Lois replied, "but I'm awfully afraid it's polio. You could have an epidemic out there."

*"You may kill me, but I am not afraid. I will
only go to heaven."*
Tona

Tragedy and Travail 10

The outbreak of polio among the Aucas was not a
total surprise. Cases had recently been reported in
less-isolated jungle tribes. Several missions, in cooperation with the Ecuadorian government, had inoculation
programs underway.

The susceptibility was among the downriver Aucas,
because the upriver people were well-fortified and in
good health. The new immigrants had not been wholly
cooperative. Many refused medicines and vitamins after recovering from the flu. Some lived out in the forest
and came into Tiwaeno only occasionally. With the
threat of an outbreak of spearing, there was little Rachel
could have done.

It was later determined that the polio virus was
brought in by a group of Quichuas. Traveling by canoe,
the Quichuas stopped first at Amoncawa's clearing on
the Curaray and shared manioc drink with the people
there, then moved up the Fish River and infected
Oncaye's immediate family at their settlement.

The second outbreak occurred at the Fish River settlement. A woman from Oncaye's group became ill and
died, foaming at the mouth, while on her way to
Tiwaeno for medical help. A man and baby were strick-
en in the same clearing and were partly paralyzed by
the time relatives got them to Tiwaeno.

A new danger loomed when Iniwa blamed Amonca-

wa's death on a downriver witch doctor and threatened
to kill the sorcerer. Iniwa, still in his teens, had been
baptized with Oncaye and Steve and Kathy Saint at
Palm Beach and had been adopted by Dayuma's
mother. In recent months, however, he had lapsed into
the old ways. Before the Christians could get to him, he
and a band of young rebels speared the witch doctor's
son. It was the first spearing in the Tiwaeno area in
twelve years.

Dayuma begged the victim's downriver relatives not
to take revenge. Then she stood watch over her foster
brother to keep him from killing the sorcerer. A week
later young Iniwa collapsed, screaming and writhing in
pain, and within hours he was dead. The Christian Aucas pronounced his death an act of God to prevent more
violence.

The deadly virus was now striking in Tiwaeno. A
nephew of Oncaye's, one of the new downriver believers, became paralyzed. "I'm going to heaven," he whispered to his unbelieving father, Tidonca, before dying.
The grief-stricken father began whittling a spear to kill
his daughter. This was what Auca fathers had done for
generations in expressing frustration over the death of a
son. Rachel happened by, grabbed the spear, and hid it
under her bed. Before the week was out, Tidonca and
two more of his family died. In his last moments, Tidonca told Dyuwi, who had been talking about the gospel
with him, "I hope to see my son in heaven."

The epidemic hit hardest among Oncaye's and
Baiwa's groups. Among those who died was the wife of
Babae, brother of Baiwa. Babae began making a spear
with the intention of killing a man to get a new spouse.
Rachel took his spear, broke it in half, and walked out of
the house without being harmed.

The witch doctor, Piyamo, was stricken, along with

one of his sons and a nephew. Kimo's nephew collapsed. As during the flue epidemic, Rachel and Dawa were up day and night, checking on patients. The difference this time was that Aucas were dying.

Rachel could feel the muscles in her arms and knees drawing up. Weak and barely able to stand, she somehow managed to keep going.

Dr. Wallace Swanson of the HCJB Shell Mera hospital and SIL nurse Lois Pederson finally flew in on September 24 with vaccine to help check the disease. They had been held up by fear of violence.

More were dead by the time they got there. But Dr. Swanson could not confirm that Rachel had been attacked by the disease.

When Kimo's nephew died on the twenty-eighth, the victim's wife, a member of Baiwa's group, smashed her husband's belongings and burned their house. When Dawa saw this, she told Rachel, "If more die, I will stop believing."

"No," Rachel said, "God calls us to be faithful unto death. You will be faithful."

Oncaye was unconscious and at the point of death. Kimo and other Christian elders anointed her with oil and prayed. Upon regaining consciousness, she spoke of having been in a beautiful place with Nimu's (Rachel's) brother. In time she recovered and showed no crippling effects of the disease.

Before the worst passed, fourteen were dead (all newcomers to Tiwaeno), and nine others were on the critical list. To keep the nine alive, Dr. Swanson built a hammock apparatus that worked like a teeter-totter, moving their diaphragms up and down as Rachel and Lois rocked them back and forth. After a few days, he had them flown to the HCJB hospital at Shell Mera, where some were placed in iron lungs. Two of the nine died there.

Medical Assistance Programs from Wheaton, Illinois, sent crutches and wheelchairs for the disabled. Nurses Margi Brothers, Gayle Johnson, and Ruth Lindskoog and physical therapist Bud Swanson, Dr. Wallace's brother, came from California to help, along with another nurse, Ruth Ann Reed, and Rosi Jung, a German midwife and new member of Wycliffe. Dr. Catherine Peeke had completed the Auca grammar for her doctoral dissertation and was now back permanently.

Rosi asked to be assigned to the Aucas to do medical work and help Rachel and Cathy Peeke with translation. A quiet, efficient, blue-eyed woman in her late thirties, she dated her conversion and call from an Allied bombing raid in which she narrowly escaped death. "When houses all around me were exploding, I realized that God was alive and if I died, I would be lost. At that time I definitely knew God wanted me to be a missionary. But I wasn't willing until I heard of the death of the five martyrs on Palm Beach. Then I accepted the call."

The terrible epidemic had subsided, but the sickness had kept the people from fields and forest. There was a terrible food shortage, and many were complaining of hunger. One day in November, Baiwa and twenty-seven other unbelievers left for their old territory, where oil rigs were now busy. Kimo caught up with them and warned that they would meet trouble. Baiwa spurned his pleas and led his group on.

Oil crews were now moving in on the ridge where it was estimated that over two hundred wild Aucas lived. Tona, the Tiwaeno teacher, had relatives there and asked that SIL pilots resume overflights. On November 20, 1969, he learned that his brother Wepe and sister Omade were living in separate clearings and that Wepe might be the real father of Oncaye. The next month he talked to Omade from a plane and asked if he would be welcome in her clearing. Speaking into the basket transmitter, she replied, "No, this is not the time. I will tell you when."

The polio patients had been moved from Shell Mera to Limoncocha, where Lois Pedersen was supervising their therapy. The young schoolteacher, Tona, flew out with Rachel to visit them and arrived while Barbara Youderian and her children were visiting from Quito.

Jerry was now fifteen and Beth was almost seventeen. Their mother had been to Tiwaeno, but they had never met any from the tribe that had killed their father. While on furlough, they had seen the film and heard Barbara speak scores of times about Palm Beach and the Aucas. Hundreds of people had pressed them with questions that they hardly knew how to answer. Beth had weathered the stress, but Jerry had become noncommunicative to the point of simply saying nothing when a question was put to him. Lately he had been giving Barbara the silent treatment. "What's troubling you, Jerry?" she would ask. "Please let me try to help you." Her only answer was silence.

Rachel saw that both Beth and Jerry met the Aucas at Limoncocha. She told them that the refusal of the five men to shoot at their attackers had helped influence the killers to become believers. She talked about how the sacrifice of their father and his friends had inspired the Aucas to risk their lives in reaching their downriver enemies. She asked them to pray for Tona, who had volunteered to take the gospel to his wild relatives on the ridge.

Jerry said nothing, but later his mother saw him walking along the grassy airstrip with Tona. They couldn't understand each other's languages, but she felt they were communicating by just being together.

While visiting at Limoncocha, Barbara caught up Wycliffe friends with news of the families of the five Palm Beach martyrs. Interest in the widows and children had never slackened among the linguists in Ecuador. "Beth will be attending North Park College in Chicago for nursing studies," Barbara said. "I'll be taking her up, I guess." Olive now had a third child, Holly. She and Walt continued to live in Deerfield, Illinois. Marilou was settled in Seattle. Her Steve would be ready for college in another year. Marj and Abe, as everyone knew, were in Quito with HCJB. Barbara said she saw Marj frequently.

Betty had recently married Dr. Addison Leitch, who was vice president of a little Presbyterian college in Missouri. He had originally invited Betty to speak at the school. His wife was then near death from cancer. Several months after his wife's death, Leitch invited Betty back to speak again, and they got better acquainted. The friendship ripened into love and marriage. Barbara had never met him, but from Betty's letters, he was a gift from the Lord—tall, masculine, and very distinguished-looking. An athlete from way back, he had played professional baseball and had coached football. He was also an excellent teacher and very brilliant intellectually, Betty said. They were all happy for Betty. Addison Leitch sounded like her kind of man.

Barbara and her two children returned to Quito. The polio patients were continuing to improve as Tona flew back to Tiwaeno, where Cathy and Rosi had remained. Rachel felt she was needed in Limoncocha a while longer. Tona was anxious to talk with his sister Omade on the ridge again. He hoped she would say it was time for him to come.

"Yes," Omade said through the radio-equipped basket when Tona was flown over, "you can come now. But you must come alone on the trail."

He understood this caution, but it would take several days to walk from Tiwaeno. An oil pilot offered to drop him, by helicopter, a short way from Omade's clearing. From there he would walk the rest of the way alone.

Bad weather delayed the flight. While waiting, Tona wrote a letter to Rachel (the first correspondence ever sent in the Auca language), recommending that the ridge people be brought first to Limoncocha for teaching from "God's Carving." "When they begin to think favorably about Father God," he said, "they can go to Tiwaeno." He was remembering the problems caused by the sudden arrival of the downriver group.

The weather cleared and the chopper whisked Tona across the jungle and dropped him with a radio about a mile from his sister's clearing. He stretched out on a dry spot, planning to spend the night and go on the next morning.

Around midnight, he heard men coming home from a hut. He caught the name Wepe and followed the men to a small house. When certain that this Wepe was his brother, he called out, "Tona, your brother has come." Wepe gave him a warm reception and told him how glad their sister, Omade, would be to see him.

Day by day Tona radioed Rachel concerning his progress in teaching "God's Carving" to his relatives. Every week or so, he asked for a plane to drop a few axes and machetes as gifts. One day he called to say that he had administered serum and saved a man bitten by a poisonous snake.

On June 5, 1970, Tona mentioned that a party was scheduled at Wepe's clearing. He might have to hide until the group dispersed. The next morning, he called again to say that he had prayed all night and believed God wanted him to remain and teach his people.

A few days later, he radioed Tiwaeno and spoke to

his mother, wife, and little daughter. He promised the little girl that with Father God's blessing, he would be home soon.

When three days passed without another call, Cathy and Dawa were flown over the clearing and saw only charred ruins. Their pilot located another clearing nearby. The houses there had also been burned to the ground. Further search flights turned up no trace of life. Tona and the ridge Aucas had disappeared.

Meanwhile, Baiwa and his group killed several oil workers, and the Ecuadorian army moved in to protect the crews. Eager to prevent more bloodshed, the oil consortium dispatched a helicopter to locate the runaways and drop Rachel and Dayuma into their clearing.

Dayuma wasted no words in warning Baiwa to get his people out of the way of oil workers and get back to the protectorate. "Here you will only meet death," she advised the old rebel. "In the protectorate you can live in peace." Baiwa reluctantly agreed to go if he could ride on a helicopter.

Nothing more was heard about Tona until around Christmas 1970, when a Wycliffe pilot and Cathy located a fresh clearing on the ridge. They saw people and dropped an electronic basket. A man who looked like Tona from the air spoke into the transmitter. Cathy thought he sounded like Tona. Suddenly a man identifying himself as Wepe broke in and said he would come with his brother back to Tiwaeno if his long-estranged daughter, Oncaye, would come and bring machetes and axes.

A chopper dropped Oncaye, her baby, and her brother Tewae. They radioed back a request that Tona and Wepe be picked up first. She and the baby and Tewae could come later.

The helicopter went in and brought two Aucas from

the ridge to an oil airstrip where a SIL plane was waiting with Cathy. The older man climbed out of the chopper and introduced himself as Wepe. He did not identify the younger one who was supposed to be Tona.

Cathy got them into the SIL plane. When they landed in Tiwaeno, Wepe stepped out and pointed to his companion. "Here is Tona."

The Aucas who had gathered around the plane looked at the young man incredulously. He obviously was not Tona. "I am Tona's mother," a woman shouted, holding up a picture. "This is not my son." The impostor turned pale.

A villager handed him a copy of Mark. "Tona was our teacher. Prove you are him by reading to us." The ridge Auca fell to the ground in fright.

Wepe pushed forward. "A witch doctor changed Tona. That's why he looks different."

"No sorcerer could do this," Dayuma declared. "You are possessed by a lying spirit. In the name of Jesus, I command it to come out." Wepe looked around in bewilderment, fear forming on his face. Then he broke and tried to run. Baiwa and some of the men started after him. "Come back," Dayuma screamed at Baiwa. "You killed my brother and my uncle. I kept you from being killed. You will not spear Wepe." The outlaws grudgingly turned around.

The pretender, who turned out to be Wepe's nephew, came back and asked to be taken home to the ridge. An oil chopper flew them out, and another chopper brought Oncaye and her child and brother back to Tiwaeno.

A call for help came from an oil-survey crew on the ridge. Aucas had speared a cook, and workers were refusing to spend another night in the area. Chopper pilot Bob Conway took out eleven frightened men. The next day, a fresh crew went in and found the cook's mutilated body.

SIL kept Ecuadorian officials up-to-date on all these happenings. In fact any government official, journalist, anthropologist, or Christian tourist who happened into Limoncocha was informed, a policy that Uncle Cam wanted the linguistic group to follow. "Let them know that we do everything in the open," he said. "When they think we're hiding something we can be in trouble." About the journalists, he counseled: "Cooperate with them. They'll make some mistakes, especially those who don't have any background of our work. But if you're friendly to them, they'll tell the world what we're doing." Uncle Cam's policy, which contrasted with some missions that kept a distance from secular journalists, was paying off. Stories about Wycliffe-SIL were appearing in *National Geographic*, *Time*, and many other widely read publications. Most were sympathetic and fairly accurate.

Stories about the continuing Auca saga were going through other channels. Rachel, Cathy, Rosi, and other Wycliffe workers described happenings in their prayer letters to home supporters. The Wycliffe press office sent out news releases to the Evangelical Press Association and many individual Christian periodicals. Rachel wrote a series of articles for the new Tyndale House publication, *Christian Times*. The names of Dawa, Oncaye, Tona, Wepe, and many other Aucas entered the vocabularies of thousands of Christians who had followed the Aucas since Palm Beach.

Some evangelical Christians continued to express feelings that Wycliffe, especially Uncle Cam, was highlighting the Aucas too much. After all, there were greater numbers of other unreached peoples in the world.

Uncle Cam was stepping down as Wycliffe's general

director, but he intended to continue as a roaming public-relations man for the Bible translation organization he had founded. He kept reminding people that over two thousand unwritten languages still beckoned, requiring eight to ten thousand more workers and a greatly widened base of financial support. He continued to believe that God was using publicity about the Aucas to help meet that goal.

A new home-support arm of Wycliffe, called Wycliffe Associates, had grown up in the United States. These "partners in Bible translation" had already sent hundreds of short-term volunteers to build houses; install electricity, water, and plumbing systems at Wycliffe centers; and do scores of other jobs for which Wycliffe linguists and support personnel had neither the time nor the talent. Wycliffe Associates was also sponsoring faith-promise banquets and other meetings at which Wycliffe members on furlough spoke. The increased financial support and new applications for membership in Wycliffe had been gratifying.

Only Dayuma among the Aucas had made public appearances in the United States, and that had been in 1957. Wycliffe Associates felt it was time for some of the transformed killers to be brought to the United States for rallies. What an attraction they would be! But more important, surely they would be a challenge to thousands.

Rachel was not eager to go. Wild Aucas still roamed on the ridge and possibly elsewhere. The mystery of the disappearance of Tona was still unsolved. Only one book of the Bible was published in Auca. How could she leave Tiwaeno? Wycliffe Associates could understand that these were valid reasons, but there were the yet-unreached tribes. God had raised up the Auca witness to challenge Christians all over the world. What better way to increase this challenge than by a series of rallies? "We'll arrange everything," Wycliffe Associates assured. "All we want you to do is come and bring some Aucas." Finally she agreed to take Kimo, Dawa, Gikita, and Sammy Padilla, who would help with interpreting and setting up equipment.

Now twenty-one and often referred to as the "civilized Auca," Dayuma's oldest son was a child of many cultures: He had been born on the hacienda, had lived a short time in the United States when he was seven, had attended Spanish-speaking school in Limoncocha and Quito, had played with Wycliffe and missionary kids, and had spent vacations among his mother's people.

The Auca Update Rallies during the spring of 1971 were some of the most newsworthy events any Christian organization had ever undertaken. Preceded by advance publicity, Rachel and the four Aucas were flown from city to city in a Cessna Skywagon and presented in press conferences before reporters and television cameras. In most of the twenty-three cities covered, the "savage killers" made the front page and the evening TV news; in New York City, they were interviewed on NBC-TV's "Today Show."

The rallies rivaled a Billy Graham crusade in crowd size and excitement. In some cities, no auditorium was large enough to hold everyone, and two or three meetings had to be held. They opened with spirited hymn singing and prayers; then the lights were turned out and a professional multimedia portrayal of Palm Beach and the miraculous happenings in Auca land was shown. The most dramatic moment of all came when the multimedia ended and Rachel, grandmotherly with graying hair drawn into a bun, stepped into a white spotlight with Uncle Gikita. Audible gasps were heard when she said, "I want to introduce you to the man who killed my brother Nate. He is now my brother in Christ." Gikita gave his testimony, with Rachel interpreting, of how he had quit killing since Jesus had changed his heart. Then Rachel presented the other Aucas. Tears flowed freely and *amens* resounded. At the end of every rally, the group received a standing ovation.

Not since the week of Palm Beach had the Aucas been so much in the news. After every appearance, hundreds pressed forward to see the celebrities close up. Many declared that what they had heard proved that Jim, Nate, Ed, Rog, and Pete had not died in vain.

Wycliffe received stacks of letters containing contributions and requests for more information about the challenge of the Bibleless tribes. Many writers described the impact of the Aucas on their lives. A typical response came from Wallace McGeehee, a Kansas City manufacturer: "Never have I witnessed any event that gave me such a spiritual uplift as did this rally. . . . It was like reading a letter from the Apostle Paul."

But, like the trip to Berlin, the bringing of Aucas to the United States for publicity did not set well with some Christians. Betty Elliot, for one, thought the appearances might have inspired American Christians but probably did the Aucas more harm than good.

The tour pace had been hectic and exhausting. For two months they saw little but airports, freeways, hotels, television stations, adoring crowds, cameras, and questioning reporters. Dawa, who had insisted on four new front teeth before she would appear in public, got sick. Kimo had seen it all before. Gikita longed for the jungle where he could hunt monkeys and toucans, although he wanted to take a television set home. The Saturday morning cartoons fascinated him. Sammy said he would never again take a trip in which there was no time to relax.

There was also concern about how the Ecuadorian government might feel about the image Americans received of that country, but apparently there were no bad effects. While the rallies were in progress, President Velasco Ibarra came again to Limoncocha and expressed appreciation for SIL's work among his country's Indian tribes, especially for the pacification of the Aucas.

Pacification was hardly complete. When Rachel and the four Aucas returned to Tiwaeno, the whereabouts of Tona was still unknown and the ridge Aucas were still giving oil people fits. With so many things pressing, including translation, Rachel was exhausted from the arduous trip. Reluctantly, she admitted to needing a rest and went home for an abbreviated furlough, her first in twelve years.

A writer for *Esquire* magazine trailed her back to Ecuador. She didn't want to see any reporter, certainly not one from what she remembered a girlie magazine like *Esquire* to be. *Esquire* writer Jerry Bledsoe convinced Don Johnson that the magazine had changed its style, however, and wangled the promise of a flight to Tiwaeno if Rachel consented. He wanted to spend at least two days there. Rachel said it was too dangerous for a man to remain overnight. She finally consented to give him an hour or two if he came out.

Bledsoe's thirteen-page article was the most comprehensive piece on the Aucas ever published by a secular magazine. He was rough on the oil companies but respectful, even friendly, to Rachel and her colleagues.

While Rachel had been away the last time, Dawa and Oncaye persuaded an oil chopper pilot to drop them on the ridge. They located Wepe and his nephew, Monga, and Wepe's half-sister, Omade. She told them that Tona had been lured into the jungle by her husband and sons and killed. The details of his murder did not come out until much later, when Dawa learned that the beloved Tiwaeno teacher had been hit in the back with an ax until he fell to the ground. He had died telling his murderers, "You may kill me, but I am not afraid. I will only go to heaven."

Dawa's brother Dyuwi (no relation to the Dyuwi at Tiwaeno), who also lived on the ridge, had been treated for snakebite by Tona and was still gravely ill. "Tona told me about Father God, but I wouldn't listen. Tell me more," he begged. Dawa gave him instruction and arranged for a helicopter to take him and his family to a landing strip. There they were picked up by SIL pilot Roy Gleason and flown into Tiwaeno. They were the first family to move from the ridge.

Soon a call for aid came from Monga, the impersonator of the martyr Tona. He claimed that Uncle Iketai, a relative of Gikita's by marriage, was dying. The oil people and SIL cooperated in taking a second ridge family to the protectorate. Then Wepe permanently moved his two wives and children to Tiwaeno.

Rachel wanted the immigration from the ridge to continue. "Let them come out a family at a time as families here are ready to receive them," she said. She met opposition from some colleagues in Ecuador who feared that the protectorate would become overpopulated. "Well, if we leave them there, we'll only invite more killings," Rachel said. The objectors gave in.

Rachel's eyes were giving her problems. She had been warned that without surgery she could go blind. Now she could hardly walk from one hut to another without stumbling over a root or a stump. One day she realized there was a new hut close by Dayuma's and Komi's house. "Who is this for?" she asked her closest Auca friend. "For you to be where I can take care of you," Dayuma replied.

Finally it became obvious to Rachel that she must get help with her cataract problem, and she went home to Pennsylvania. By the time she got there, she was too blind to walk across the street by herself.

The surgery on her right eye was a success, but she was reminded that her other eye remained a problem. She was unwilling to remain any longer, however. She felt the Aucas were more important than her health.

Taking Inventory 11

"**W**hy try to change the culture of the Aucas? Why not let them be happy as they are?" How many times had Wycliffe members heard this question from well-meaning journalists and visitors to Ecuador and other fields?

"To say 'They're happy, leave them alone' is ridiculous," Don Johnson told *Esquire's* Jerry Bledsoe. "People who say primitive people are happy aren't near enough to know them. . . . Change is inevitable. We want to help them make this change as smoothly and as untraumatically as possible."

"Our mission here," explained Dr. Glen Turner, SIL's tribal affairs director in Ecuador, to Georgie Ann Geyer from the *Chicago Daily News*, "is not to change their culture but to change their desires so they will want to do good to their neighbors. Unless help is given to the Aucas, they can't stand up to the contact. It's not change, but the speed of change."

Change was the nub of the problem in the 1970s. The Aucas were squarely in the path of onrushing civilization, represented by big oil and land-hungry homesteaders.

The record of what had happened to other tribal groups was plain and grim. North American Indians, pushed into reservations where they became the serfs of welfarism, suffered abysmally high rates of suicide and alcoholism. Brazil's Indian population was down from several million to little more than two hundred thousand. Every missionary, linguist, and anthropologist could cite examples of the white man's cruelty in exploiting and oppressing ethnic minorities. Perhaps the worst cruelty of all was robbing peoples of their traditions, languages, and dignity.

The oil consortium provided the easiest target for criticism. Yet the critics often failed to mention that big oil was in partnership with the Ecuadorian government, which was trying to lift the national economy. Their motive was not to exterminate the Aucas but to pacify and educate them and bring them into the system. This was why the government was eager to cooperate with SIL among the Aucas and other minorities of the country. SIL, informed officials knew, was helping the Aucas survive the inevitable culture collision despite some unfounded charges that the linguists were in league with oil companies and "American imperialism."

The oil people had their job to do and wanted the troublesome Aucas out of the way. So they kept in close radio contact with Tiwaeno and provided helicopters when needed to move wild Indians from areas where crews were working.

They took every precaution imaginable, yet attacks continued. On April 4, 1972, about dusk, a crew of oil workers was resting in a tent on the ridge. Without warning, about twenty naked Aucas wearing feather headdresses leaped out of the jungle and began hurling spears. Two brothers nearest the front of the tent rolled under their cots, seriously wounded. Another oil worker ran out waving an unloaded shotgun and frightened the marauders away. A radio operator at Limoncocha picked up the emergency call and dispatched a rescue plane to bring the wounded there for medical treatment.

The wild Aucas knew only that outsiders were encroaching on their territory. They attacked oil crews for the same reason the men from Dayuma's clan had attacked the missionaries on Palm Beach: they perceived them as enemies to be repelled.

The *Esquire* writer noted that Wycliffe members had spent endless hours dealing with problems created by the oil push, time they could have used for language study and Bible translation. "Can you think of anything good that oil has done?" he asked Rachel.

Rachel concluded that oil had been helpful on one score: "It forced us all into contact with the rest of the Aucas long before we would have had the courage to tackle it. . . . [The Christian Aucas] knew their relatives would kill the oil company people and they wanted to protect them. They also knew that . . . their people . . . would die from the outside sicknesses brought in, plus wanting all along to teach them about the Lord. So if you look at the all-over picture, maybe oil has done us a favor." Rachel didn't want to berate the oil companies. "I will say that the companies have in general been very cooperative."

Dealing with the oil crews and the provocation they provided by just being in Auca country was not the only problem. Settlers came in behind them. In 1962 the government census counted 79,007 in the eastern jungle region. By 1974 the population had increased to 168,000. Many newcomers had established homesteads right on the edge of the Auca Protectorate. A few were living inside the outer reaches of the protectorate. The Aucas in the protectorate were upset, and some were suggesting that the encroachers should be taught a lesson. Rachel and her colleagues tried to calm those wanting to attack with assurances that SIL would notify the government and the intruding settlers would have to pull up stakes and move back.

The Aucas handled it themselves, however, by destroying the gardens of the encroachers. Hunters and fishermen were more difficult to manage. Some sneaked in, took their prey, and were gone before they were noticed. Some traded outside goods: pots, transistor radios, machetes, and other items to Aucas for informal permission to hunt and fish inside the protectorate. With guns and big nets, the outsiders took a heavy toll on wildlife. Dynamite and DDT were even more devastating to the ecological balance that had held for centuries. Fish and other aquatic life forms were virtually wiped out in some streams. Auca hunters and fishermen had to walk farther and farther for good fishing and hunting.

The settlers and foragers were mostly Quichuas. Other kinds of visitors came because of the notoriety of the Aucas. For many years, visitors had been confined to missionaries, journalists, government officials, and reputable scholars. Now that the oil companies had landing strips and helipads all over the jungle, tourists could skip in and out with ease.

Dayuma's son, Sammy, who was well known in Quito, became a sort of tour guide. He took clients wherever they wanted to go, even to the ridge where about one hundred wild Aucas still remained. A German journalist made a trip in with Sammy and wrote a bitterly anti-missionary book based more on bias than fact. He reported finding machine gun bullets on Palm Beach—evidence, he suggested, that cast a shadow on the motives of the five slain missionaries. The bullets— if he actually found any—were undoubtedly fired by the military rescue party when they sprayed the jungle to warn possible attackers away while the bodies were being recovered.

There was no way the visitors could be stopped or Aucas kept from going outside. For one thing, the Indians were now scattered across the protectorate. Since around 1970, the Auca people had been moving farther out from Tiwaeno to where food prospects were better. Without a knowledge of scientific agriculture, a field could be cultivated only for two or three years, then new land had to be found and cleared. The ducks, turkeys, and small herd of cows that Rachel had helped obtain were not sufficient.

Within a few years there were six distinct settlements in the protectorate. Dayuma and Komi lived near Palm Beach with about one hundred fifty people. Dawa and Kimo were on the Tzapino River, a little nearer Tiwaeno, with around one hundred. Dyuwi and Oba remained at Tiwaeno with about the same number. The other three settlements were smaller.

Sunday services were held in most of these settlements after the form instituted by Dayuma at Tiwaeno. Rachel, Cathy, and Rosi did not travel but stayed at Tiwaeno. Their main task continued to be Bible translation.

But what good would Scripture be without readers? Over the years, Rachel had held reading classes. Dayuma and Dyuwi had helped. Tona had been the brightest hope as a teacher before he was killed. Literacy had lagged since his death.

Patricia Kelley, a new SIL member of Wycliffe, was assigned to set up and coordinate a literacy program among the Aucas. She taught the women and children during the day and the men at night while on the lookout for especially bright students who could be taken to Limoncocha for teacher training. The ultimate goal was a bilingual school similar to those initiated by SIL in other language groups. Aucas would teach Aucas. Students would first learn to read and write their own language, then they would move into Spanish.

While SIL was stepping up literacy training efforts, a Brethren missionary, Lloyd Rogers, at Dayuma's request, obtained government permission to begin a school with a Quichua Christian teacher near Dayuma's and Komi's settlement. Quichua preachers had already been coming in to hold services and baptize new believers. Jim Elliot had led Gervacio Cerda, one of the preachers, to Christ when Gervacio was a boy. When Jim was killed on Palm Beach, Gervacio recommitted his life to Christ and later became pastor of the Quichua congregation at Limoncocha. Gervacio held an evangelistic crusade for the Aucas; recalling the sacrifice of the missionaries, he implored the unconverted to accept the gospel for which the five had died. Around fifty responded.

The Wycliffe workers had mixed feelings about the educational and evangelistic thrust of the Brethren among the Aucas. They rejoiced in the spiritual results, but they feared that the Auca Christians might become subservient to the Quichua church and lose their cultural and linguistic identity. They noticed with concern that when Quichuas were present, Aucas hesitated to participate in church services. It was obvious they felt inferior.

Wycliffe-SIL policy called for linguistic analysis and translation supported by educational, medical, and community development work as might be needed. Members did not organize churches or perform other clergy roles. These responsibilities were passed on to local Christians, national church bodies, and regular missionaries.

The Auca work had been atypical within Wycliffe from the start. It was customary for a married couple or two single linguists of the same sex to work together in a tribe. Rachel and a non-Wycliffe member had been together until 1963. From 1963 until 1969, Rachel had pretty much operated on her own. The other strong presence was Dayuma, who exercised great influence on her people because of her knowledge from the outside and instruction from Rachel. After 1969, when Dr. Cathy Peeke took up regular residence in Tiwaeno, Rachel and Dayuma continued to be the strongest personalities among the group.

Rachel was by far the best known of the more than seventy Wycliffe members assigned to Ecuador. She was now quite popular in evangelical Christian circles in the United States, especially among Wycliffe's supporting constituency. This was not, of course, by her own choosing, but because of the Auca Update Rallies, the numerous articles published about her and the Aucas in the Christian press, *The Dayuma Story*, and the newest Harper book, written by her friend Ethel Wallis, *Aucas Downriver*.

The Wycliffe group in Ecuador, like other SIL field branches, was autonomous. The group elected its own officers and committees, assigning members to tasks befitting their talents and sense of calling. Rachel's situation was somewhat unique; she had worked much more independently than many of her colleagues.

Everyone had the highest respect and admiration for Rachel. None of her colleagues questioned her motives. They simply felt that it was time for a new look at the Aucas in view of SIL policies and its contractual agreement with the government. Decisions should be made about what should be done in the future. The rapid change precipitated by the oil companies made this a necessity. The next few years would be critical for the Aucas' survival as a viable society.

There was another consideration that could not be ignored. Uncle Cam's old friend Velasco Ibarra was no longer in the presidential palace. Bridges of mutual understanding and cooperation had to be built with the new government. Nothing could be taken for granted. The Aucas had always been famous in Ecuador. With the new oil fields and the population push eastward, a spate of stories about the tribe was appearing in newspapers and magazines. All sorts of groups were interested in the Aucas, and some were suspicious of foreign missionaries and technical aid missions, the designation given to SIL. Already there were attacks in newspapers in Peru and Colombia, and a few critical articles had appeared in Ecuador. It was more essential than ever that Wycliffe's work be open and beyond informed criticism. The Auca work especially would have to bear the closest scrutiny.

Dr. Jim Yost, who held a Ph.D. in anthropology, and his wife, Kathie, were assigned to the Aucas. The bearded red-head's doctorate was from the University of Colorado. Before that, he and Kathie had studied at Northwestern College, the alma mater of Roger Youderian. They often saw Roger's portrait on a wall in the administration building with an inscription about his martyrdom on Palm Beach; but the couple had known little about the Aucas until coming to Ecuador in 1973. Jim was assigned to do an anthropological field study of the Aucas and make recommendations for the future. Kathie would have her hands full with their young daughter but would assist him as much as possible.

Rachel agreed to cooperate with the study but voiced her fears about Jim's safety as the first Wycliffe man to live among the Aucas. "There are still plenty of unredeemed killers left," she warned. "I won't be responsible for anything that happens to you."

After becoming conversant with the language, Jim began moving among the Auca settlements—including living for a short time among the wild Aucas on the ridge—asking questions, taking family histories, observing, making extensive notes, and building on information provided by Betty Elliot, Rachel, Cathy, and Rosi. The complete field study took three years.

In 1976, a team of six other scientists, including another anthropologist, two medical professors from the Duke University Medical Center, and two dentists from the University of Toronto Faculty of Dentistry, participated with Jim in an intensive, four-week medical analysis of the Aucas. They examined and took medical histories from 147 males and 146 females, about 60 percent of the population. Among their startling finds:

No baldness or color blindness.

Only six dull persons: two had sustained head trauma, another was affected by fever, and one had Down's Syndrome.

No hypertension. The highest blood pressure reading was 109 on the systolic (upper) scale.

No cardiovascular problems of consequence.

No hypothyroidism.

High fertility among women. Only one in fifty-nine married women of child-bearing age claimed she had been unable to conceive. Male fertility was hard to determine because of sexual promiscuity, principally stemming from the tradition that a man was entitled to cohabit with his wife's sisters.

The one major health problem was tooth decay. Out of 230 examined, 225 had bad teeth. The dentist could find no explanation for this inasmuch as the Aucas had little access to salt, sugar, and processed foods.

From oral histories compiled by Jim for six generations back, they calculated these causes of mortality among the Aucas:

Intertribal spearings	61%
Shot by outsiders	13%
Various illnesses	12%
Snakebite	4%
Infants buried alive	4%
Unknown	6%

The almost complete cessation of spearings, except on the ridge, was obviously the biggest reason for the dramatic population increase during recent years.

The team brought in $6,000 worth of donated drugs. They used only a fraction of the medicines because 95 percent of the Indians checked were "very robust and in excellent health with no evidence of malnutrition." (Only six persons were still affected by severe paralysis from the polio epidemic of six years before.)

The team suggested several reasons for the unusually good health of the Aucas:

A nutritious balanced diet of proteins from game and fish, carbohydrates from domestic crops, and vitamins and minerals from crops, fruits, and nuts.

Medical treatment by SIL workers and special health teams. For seventeen years the foreign linguists had routinely provided free medicines from their own allowances, supplemented by occasional donations from the government and other agencies.

The hostile environment in which only the fittest had survived—the physical habitat of the jungle

and the social milieu in which defective babies
were usually killed. By killing off the unfit, genetic
diseases had been kept down in a population that
practiced close inbreeding.

With outsiders pressing in, the medical specialists
could not give an optimistic prognosis for the future.
They noted that scabies and upper-respiratory infec-
tions, common among the Quichuas, were now showing among the Aucas. Other outside diseases would
probably be brought in as contact increased.

In 1977, a measles epidemic hit Quichua settlements
and spread into the protectorate. Despite a pre-
epidemic vaccination program, nearly 10 percent of the
Aucas were stricken, and of these 90 percent developed
secondary pneumonia. Aware that measles had taken
heavy tolls in other jungle tribes, SIL pilots flew in extra
antibiotics and other medications. Not one Auca died,
and the epidemic subsided.

Of course, Dr. Jim Yost's study encompassed much
more than health. He tried to look at the total picture—
past, present, and future—and make recommendations
that he thought would best help the much-publicized
Aucas not only survive physically but also preserve
their cultural and spiritual identities against the perils of
increased contact with outsiders.

He noted that the speed of change was picking up. In
1977, only ten Auca men were working in the oil fields.
A year later, this number had more than tripled. There
had been several intermarriages with Quichuas, result-
ing in the formation of new kinship alliances. Aucas
were walking out to stores in Arajuno and staying overnight with new Quichua kin. The Quichuas, in turn,
were visiting their new Auca relatives and feeling free
to hunt and fish in Auca territory. This was causing

hard feelings among Aucas not linked by marriage to outsiders.

Ever since the first introduction of outside goods, the Aucas had been fascinated by the products of outsiders. Machetes were especially cherished, for the Aucas had only flint knives for sharpening spears and cutting. On hunting trips, when they had come across an occasional stone ax, they had said, "Only God could make this."

Rachel, Betty, and Dayuma brought more treasures from the outside world. The Auca women saw how much better aluminum pots were than clay utensils. They admired and ogled Dayuma's sewing machine, which could make a garment in a few hours. Everything the foreigners had fascinated them. The linguists saw what this could lead to and limited imports, even after flight service began.

Sharing among kinspeople had always been taken for granted in the tribe. One could simply take whatever he needed without asking. The first Aucas to walk out to Arajuno did this in a store and couldn't understand why the owner got angry. But they quickly caught on to the ways of the outside world and began bringing smoked meat and fish, blowguns, and other items for exchange. Transistor radios, candy, gum, and decorated clothing came to Aucaland. Caps like those the SIL pilots wore were especially popular among the young men.

As an anthropologist, Jim Yost recognized another, more-worrisome syndrome of a long-isolated tribal group interacting with the civilized world for the first time. Many Aucas were ashamed of who they were. They wanted to live down their past and be accepted. This was one reason the Aucas wanted to wear clothes (another was for protection of the body). Yet they could not melt into the population. For one thing, long hair could hardly disguise the drooping ear lobes that had once held the traditional balsa plugs. Whenever they went into an outside town, people stared and giggled, and some Aucas ran to hide.

All of this and Auca servility to Christian Quichuas in church services suggested to Jim that the Aucas were on the downward path that so many tribes in North and South America had trod.

The process, so familiar to anthropologists, began with a sense of deprivation, inferiority, and shame. Efforts to overcome this deprivation by adopting the ways of the other culture led to disorientation in which members of a group did not know who they were. The next step downward was demoralization, followed by disintegration of the society.

Jim believed the Aucas had not yet passed the first stage. Most still held to the best of the old traditions. The elimination of spearing and infanticide by the Christians had been accomplished internally by the permeation of the gospel, with some influence by the linguists. The Aucas possessed land, though Jim thought the protectorate was not large enough for all. They still lived by the traditional subsistence economy. Their diet was adequate, their health good, and they had access to modern medicine. For the most part, Aucas still had control over their lives.

But the future did not look good. Whether the Aucas would be run over by civilization or survive as a people, he believed would depend to a large degree on how SIL fulfilled its stewardship trust from the national government.

He included these recommendations in his report to his colleagues in Ecuador:

1. Stop using the name *Auca*, the Quichua word for "savage," and call them by the name they gave them-

selves, *Waorani*, meaning "the people."

2. Withdraw SIL workers from the protectorate for a time so the Waorani can learn better to stand alone. Upon returning, workers should spread out among the settlements and not concentrate in Tiwaeno. More translation should be done in Limoncocha with Waorani assistants.

3. Help the Waorani develop a political structure that would not destroy their traditional egalitarian form of society. This would not be easy; there had to be spokesmen to deal with government officials and other authority figures from outside.

4. Stop the migration from the ridge, at least until more land could be secured and newcomers could fend for themselves without becoming dependent on relatives in the protectorate.

While recognizing the enormous contribution Dayuma had made to the tribe's spiritual and physical welfare, Jim suggested that she had made the people too dependent on her. A balance needed to be restored, with other Waorani, especially men, taking more leadership.

The SIL branch discussed Jim's recommendations in great detail. Rachel vigorously defended Dayuma's role. She cited "honorific pronouns" used in reference to women as evidence that female leadership was in the tradition of the tribe, although she believed that men should be the heads of households and the leaders of the church.

Rachel felt strongly that SIL should continue to assist families wanting to move from the ridge as their relatives were able to receive them. "We promised them they could all come," she reminded. "We'll be going back on our word." Rachel also warned that leaving wild ones on the ridge would be inviting further attacks on oil workers.

Rachel further objected to restrictions on the residence of SIL workers among the Aucas. "After living with the Aucas for almost twenty years, at least twelve years alone, I don't think I can treat them like a visiting anthropologist."

The discussion continued. All were honestly seeking what they thought was best for the future of the Waorani. Many paused to praise Rachel for her long and sacrificial commitment to the group that had killed her brother. However, in the end, the majority adopted Jim's recommendations in principle and asked everyone to cooperate.

A more pressing personal problem loomed for Rachel. She was now almost blind in her left eye. In June 1979, she flew to St. Petersburg, Florida, for more surgery. The doctor removed the clouded cataract from this eye and implanted a tiny calibrated lens. Later, he said, she could have a soft lens put on her other eye.

After the surgery, she spent several weeks resting, then flew to Wycliffe's International Linguistics Center in Dallas. Here she is sharing her vast knowledge of Auca lore with new trainees being readied for assignments to yet-unreached language minorities.

Rachel is now approaching sixty-six. Her hair, which was always light, is quite gray. Her eyesight is vastly improved. Her step is still firm under her portly frame. Her recall of Aucas is sharp and clear, but she must peg dates to events. "You don't live by the calendar among the Aucas," she says.

She worries about "my people." The recent killing of three Quichua oil workers on the ridge concerns her. "I told them that would happen if they left the wild Aucas back there."

Retirement is out of the question. She'd like to return

and live with the Aucas, "where I feel at home." Many Wycliffe friends believe she could have a greater ministry in the homeland, giving the challenge to reach the rest of the Bibleless tribes.

In Tiwaeno and other settlements in the protectorate, people constantly ask about her. "How is Nimu?" Dyuwi wonders. "Are her eyes well? When is she coming back?"

They also still ask about Betty Elliot. "Where is Gikari?" Dawa inquires. "What is she doing? If you see her, tell her we are believing in God and living well."

"To God be the glory, great things He has done."
Fanny Crosby

What Hath God Wrought? 12

We were a young Southern Baptist pastor and wife serving a small church in a dingy corner of New Orleans when the Auca massacre occurred. We had never heard of the five missionaries and their missions and knew only what we read in the papers. Like millions of others, we admired their courage and were challenged by their sacrifice, yet we needed confirmation of God's purpose in this seeming tragedy. When a denominational leader stopped by, we asked his opinion.

"Tragic, tragic waste," he said, shaking his head. "They were fine young men, but headstrong and impulsive. They should have waited." Then he added with a smugness that rankled us, "Our missionaries would never have gone in there."

Was Palm Beach a tragedy that never should have happened? Did the five missionaries die needlessly in a foolhardy venture? Has the Auca experience been blown out of proportion by the media, both evangelical and secular—magnified and sensationalized to ridiculous extremes?

These questions deserve sober consideration.

An oft-mentioned rumination is that the five should have left the Aucas to Rachel Saint and Wycliffe. Wy-

cliffe had never lost a single linguist in making contacts
with tribes known to be hostile to outsiders (a record
that stands today). Rachel knew firsthand about the entry to the headhunting Shapras in neighboring Peru.
But they chose to keep the operation from Wycliffe for
reasons noted earlier.

Another hindsight observation, which is unfair, is
that they failed to learn from the killing of five New
Tribes missionaries in Bolivia, twelve years before. Two
brothers, Cecil and Bob Dye; Dave Bacon; George Hos-
bach; and Eldon Hunter set off, unarmed, to contact the
Ayores, a tribe as notorious as the Aucas. These five
were every bit as concerned about the spiritual welfare
of the Ayores as Jim Elliot and his comrades would be
about the Aucas in the next decade. A Bolivian official
warned them: "The Ayores attack any civilized person
who comes near them—slip up and club victims in their
hammocks. You'll never come back alive." When they
didn't return in a month, a search party went after them
and found only some of their belongings. Not until
around 1950 did their families and fellow missionaries
learn the circumstances of their deaths. The men of an
Ayore village had killed them while their chief was
away. Upon returning, the chief saw the bodies and
scolded the warrior for killing visitors whom he believed to have been descendants of a legendary white
ancestor. Had he been present, the five New Tribes
missionaries might have been received with goodwill.

The Bolivian incident went largely unnoticed at the
time. A book, *God Planted Five Seeds*, was later written
by Jean Dye Johnson, one of the widows, and published
in 1966 in the Harper "Jungle Classics" series that had
been initiated by massive public interest in the Palm
Beach massacre.

The Palm Beach Five knew about these killings and

the martyrdom of a sixth New Tribes worker in Bolivia in 1951 who was set upon while living alone in the territory of hostile Nhambiquara Indians.

The five in Ecuador did not go wholly on blind faith. They did try to learn a little of the language. They did drop gifts in an effort to establish goodwill and prepare the Aucas for face-to-face contact. They did take guns to frighten off attackers. They did build a tree house as a fortress at night. They did everything deemed possible while keeping the operation a secret.

With all this, they realized the great risk they were taking. They willingly, even joyfully, took this risk in obedience to Christ's commission. They were absolutely committed to being at His disposal. As Jim Elliot wrote during his senior year of college:

> What is this, Lord Jesus, that Thou shouldst make
> an end
> Of all that I possess, and give Thyself to me?
> So that is nothing now to call my own
> Save Thee; Thyself alone my treasure.
> Taking all, Thou givest full measure of Thyself
> With all things else eternal—
> Things unlike the mouldy pelf by earth possessed.
> But as to life and godliness—all things are mine
> And in God's garments dressed I am
> With Thee, an heir to riches in the spheres divine.
> Strange, I say, that suffering loss
> I have so gained everything in getting
> Me a friend who bore a cross.

These men were neither the first nor the last evangels of the gospel to die for the commitment that has sent disciples of Christ, oblivious to danger and personal risk, into the fray and competition for the hearts and souls of the unredeemed. Jim, Nate, Ed, Rog, and Pete

went in the spirit of first-century deacon Stephen and
myriads of martyrs since. Hindsight observations of
what might have been can be made of all: If Stephen
had only used more tact in his address to the Sanhedrin;
if John Huss had stayed out of Bohemian politics; if the
188 evangelical martyrs of the Boxer Rebellion in China
during the summer of 1900 had heeded warnings of the
step-up of antiforeign terrorism and moved to safer
cities; if the New Tribes missionaries in Bolivia had been
more cautious and waited longer; if Jim, Nate, Ed, Rog,
and Pete had. . . .

If every precaution had been observed by every disciple of Christ in every dangerous situation, there would
probably be no church today.

A statement attributed to Tertullian, "Blood of the
martyrs is the seed of the Church," is both fact and
prophecy. History is full of examples. The church of the
early centuries was borne along by rivers of blood until
it became the religion of the Roman Empire. The Protestant Reformation flamed from the fires built around
such martyrs as John Huss. Protestants more than doubled in China during the six years following the Boxer
massacres. The church in South Korea, which experienced bitter persecution and lost thousands of martyrs
to the Communists, is now the largest visible church in
Asia.

The principle also holds for purity and strength.
Historians find that Christians are likely to be most loyal
and dedicated in places where the cost for living out
their faith is greatest.

What has God wrought from the martyrdom of Jim
Elliot, Nate Saint, Ed McCully, Pete Fleming, and Roger
Youderian? In the early part of this book, we narrated
the immediate and short-range impact in Ecuador and
the larger Christian world: the flood of articles and

books; the memorial services and mass rallies; the rush of young people offering themselves as replacements in the missionary ranks for the five who died in Palm Beach.

Why didn't the martyrdom in 1944 of the five New Tribes missionaries in Bolivia have as much force? Five young missionaries disappeared while trying to contact Indians just as notorious as the Aucas. Three had families, one was newly wed. A dramatic search got underway. Other parallels could be cited. What did the Auca massacre have that the Ayore killings didn't?

Two differences appear central. Consider the times. The New Tribes men disappeared in November 1944; the search party was not launched until December, for the five had told two colleagues privy to the expedition not to come looking for them for a month. At this time, Allied forces were advancing on all fronts of World War II, bringing the most exciting and encouraging news of the war. The media and the Allied world were preoccupied with battlefield heroics and victories. By comparison, the disappearance of five missionaries in a backward little South American country was considered of little importance, even if the media had known what was happening. They didn't.

In contrast, the Palm Beach incident came during a quiet time, when little of news value was happening in the world. About the only other news that week was the announced engagement of Grace Kelly and Prince Rainier and a raise in the wage scale of New York plumbers to $3.75 an hour.

The second difference was communications. Palm Beach had HCJB, Cornell Capa, and V. Raymond Edman. The missionary radio station with a worldwide reach disseminated the gripping story and served as a press agency for other media interested in the story.

Capa put the story in *Life*, the most popular picture magazine of that era, and initiated the swell of books. Edman channeled stories to both evangelical and secular media.

Did evangelicals discover the mass media, or did the mass media discover evangelicals? Probably it was a combination of both, with the result being the most publicized missionary incident of all time.

Of course, this is all human reasoning. What secular man calls chance the believer credits to providence. The right people were in place at the right time for the world to be informed, the church shaken, and millions of Christians challenged as perhaps they had never been before. "Shouldn't we merely acknowledge," asks Charles Bennett, current president of MAF, "that God chose to use the media for His purposes?"

Once the communication links were opened, the story continued. Again, whether by chance or design, human agency was involved: Cornell Capa; President Edman; Uncle Cam Townsend; Harper, a secular publisher; editors; writers; promoters; Billy Graham; the widows, especially Betty Elliot; Rachel Saint; Wycliffe Bible Translators. The publicity was worth millions if a monetary tag had been attached—publicity that gave the world a new image of evangelical Christianity as a force that could turn a tribe of killers into peaceful, compassionate human beings. That publicity disturbed and irritated religious liberals, and some evangelicals as well, who wondered why Christians couldn't get as excited about race discrimination and ghettos at home and international peace.

The Auca event in totality has undoubtedly had its greatest influence on the small church bodies in the National Association of Evangelicals, the core constituency of Billy Graham, Youth for Christ, World Vision, the independent evangelical colleges and seminaries, the mission societies that the *Christian Century* loved to castigate, Wycliffe Bible Translators, and other agencies and groups arising principally from the fundamentalist reaction to liberal Protestantism of the 1920s and '30s.

Unfortunately, no scientific study has been made to assess the impact across this segment of Christianity that has grown much faster than mainline American denominations during recent years. It would be interesting to know how many pastors, teachers, missionaries, and other Christian workers were decisively influenced in their youth by the Auca event. Perhaps some day an evangelical foundation will undertake such a vast research project.

Wheaton College would be a good starting point. Two dorms there are named after Jim Elliot and Nate Saint, and the athletic field is named after Ed McCully. Students know them only from books and materials. Older faculty members and retired teachers who still live in the town (Dr. Edman retired in 1965 and is now dead) remember Elliot best. Dr. Arthur Volle and his wife were houseparents in the dorm now named for Jim. "Jim and his roommate David Howard cleaned the washrooms and hallways. They made the floors and walls sparkle—just sparkle." Volle, a former dean and now a counselor, recalls that toward the end of his senior year, Jim got up before his class and asked their forgiveness for being judgmental of some he had considered less spiritual than himself. "After that, he kind of loosened up. At the Senior Sneak he did a little square dancing, which at that time was a big taboo at Wheaton. But he was always a good guy." Ed Coray, retired athletic director, chuckles over the time Jim rode a mule up the main hall of the administration building. Paul Bechtel, retired from the English department, remembers

Jim as "a really remarkable fellow who lived a very
rigorous life."

On the second floor of the administration building,
there is a large wallboard listing by year of graduation
the names of Wheaton alumni who are missionaries.
Jim's, Ed's, and Nate's have stars by them, indicating
they are dead.

A count of names on the wall reveals two periods
when there was an upsurge in missionaries—from 1947-
50 and from 1957-59. The first rise can be accounted for
by the veterans who received their calls during World
War II. The second increase probably was a response to
the Auca massacre. Since the class of '59, which sent
fifty-five to the mission field, there has been a steady
decrease in numbers. From 1965-70, missionary commitments have averaged less than 25 per class.

From scores of interviews in Ecuador and the U.S.
and research into files at Wheaton College and elsewhere, we ran across numerous stories about people
who were touched in a significant way by the Auca
experience. Sam Saint, for example, spoke at a church
in Rochester, New York. Mark Anderson, the pastor's
young son, sketched a plane, himself, and a stream on a
piece of brown paper and wrote underneath, "Tonight I
told Jesus I would do whatever He wanted me to do."
Mark now serves with Campus Crusade's Athletes in
Action ministry. Rachel Saint says she has never spoken
anywhere "where somebody didn't come up and say,
'God spoke to me through what happened on Palm
Beach or with the Aucas.' When I was in Minnesota
recently for my nephew Phillip's wedding, a man came
into the pastor's home from off the street, asking for
me. He said, 'You don't know me, but I know you.
When I was nine years old my mother woke me up to
pray for the five men who were missing.' He went on to

say he had applied to Wycliffe but was not accepted because of some personal complications." After 25 years, all widows report similar experiences almost everywhere they go and speak.

Russell Hitt, longtime editor of *Eternity* magazine who before his retirement was distinguished for many books, wrote the biography of Nate Saint. "This was my first book, and I was scared to death," he says. "My future books were better, I think, but none ever got near the response that *Jungle Pilot* did. Ten or fifteen years after the book was out, a friend of mine, Charles Troutman, did a survey of missionaries in the Latin America Mission. As I recall, thirty-four people in that group said *Jungle Pilot* had been the means. That's only one mission, certainly not the largest in our evangelical world."

The shadow of Nate Saint is especially long among Mission Aviation Fellowship and Jungle Aviation and Radio Service, the air arm of Wycliffe-SIL. The house that Nate built still stands at Shell Mera across from the hangar that shelters MAF planes. Tim Cooper, one of the MAF pilots, lives in the Saint house; and his wife operates the radio in the same nook in which Marj sat waiting for Nate's call that never came. They entertain a steady stream of Christian tourists who want to see the house and the furniture that remains from the time of Nate and Marj. The table around which the widows sat when they received the details of the killings from Dr. Art Johnston has been moved upstairs. Tim is the son of Dave Cooper, now in Brazil. Dave was the missionary at the University of Oklahoma who first told Jim Elliot about the Aucas.

"The outstanding monument to Nate is the alternate emergency fuel system," Tim notes. "It's much more refined now, but the main idea was Nate's. Our logs from various fields show a number of documented 'saves' due to the alternate system."

One has no difficulty finding pilots and mechanics in both MAF and Wycliffe who were influenced by Nate and *Jungle Pilot*. Paul Duffy, as a boy, made a little bucket like the one Nate used in his drops and hung over his desk. Years later, Paul became a SIL pilot in Ecuador and made many flights to Tiwaeno. He is now at JAARS headquarters in Waxhaw, North Carolina, partially paralyzed from a crash. Al Meehan was a policeman in Baltimore when he read *Jungle Pilot*. After training at the Moody Bible Institute's Aviation School, he began flying for Wycliffe in Ecuador.

From interviews and by mail, we received many testimonials from missionaries who knew we were writing this book. We can only quote from a few.

Margie Fairweather, serving with her pilot husband under MAF in Zaire, heard the call: "My family comes from Marj Saint's home church in Idaho. I remember quite plainly sitting around the table just after a telephone call from Marj's dad saying there wasn't much hope of finding the fellows alive. I knew God was asking me, 'Margie, are you willing?' I answered yes, even though I was only a sophomore in high school."

Ted Jones, with Wycliffe in Mexico, said: "I was a high school senior in Princeton, Illinois, in 1956. I was lying on my bed, listening to Bob Savage of HCJB give a very detailed account of what had happened and also challenging young people to take the place of the five who had died. I remember being deeply touched, and I was left with an impression that stayed with me for a long time."

George Boggs has logged almost 10,000 hours of flying time for MAF in Laos, the Philippines, and West Kalimantain (Borneo): "I was already a pilot when the five were killed and could hardly sleep with the burden of 'perhaps they really need us to take Nate Saint's place?' With three children and one due that very month, my wife, Fran, said, 'Why don't you go over to MAF and see?' "

Hope Hurlbut, a Canadian translator with Wycliffe in Malaysia, wrote: "The news of the martyrs made me really search my heart to see whether or not I was willing to suffer as a martyr, if the Lord so desired. It was one of the things that confirmed my resolve to go at all costs and to stay at all costs."

Erma Wiens is with the Gospel Missionary Union in Italy. Her husband, Arthur, was a classmate of Jim Elliot and Ed McCully at Wheaton, and his name was found on Jim's prayer list in a notebook taken from his trousers. Erma told of another life changed: "Valeria, a sixteen-year-old Italian girl, read about the martyrs in an Italian news magazine and wrote the president of Ecuador. He forwarded her letter to Betty Elliot, and Betty put her in touch with us. She said she was wasting her life and wanted to help Betty. We helped her to become a Christian and enrolled her in a Bible correspondence course. She subsequently became a full-time member of our staff and worked with us in preparing Christian literature for children. She and I coauthored a Bible-story book that is now sold all over Italy."

Charles R. Swindoll, pastor of the First Evangelical Free Church in Fullerton, California, largest congregation in his denomination, told us: "It was that particular event that turned my life around and rearranged my career as I got into the ministry."

Wayne Detzler, a former executive with Greater Europe Mission and now pastor of the Baptist church in Kensington, England, said: "I was thinking seriously of missions prior to that time, but this was one of the elements that pushed me over the edge to become a missionary. Many of us at Wheaton sort of felt we had to take up the torch those guys were forced to put down. We obviously didn't all go to South America, but we went all over the world."

Judy Maxwell, Wycliffe member in Ecuador, had her life changed: "I came with my daughter from England in 1963 to take a job at the British Embassy in Quito. I was full of bitterness and resentment over the breakup of my marriage and had tried one religion after another without finding what I needed. In Quito I met Marj Saint. She invited me to see the film 'Through Gates of Splendor.' I asked if I could visit the Aucas, and she arranged that. I saw what Christ had done for them and how Marj and Rachel had forgiven the killers of their loved ones. After returning to Quito, I accepted Christ in a friend's office. I am a Christian today and serving Him full-time because of what happened on Palm Beach and among the Aucas."

Ron Ehrenberg, a Wycliffe pilot in Colombia, described the event's effect: "I was flying with the USAF, shortly after I became a Christian, when *Jungle Pilot* spoke to my heart. It was truly a major influence in my life."

Ian M. Hay, general director of the Sudan Interior Mission, was touched: "I was a new missionary in Nigeria at the time, and the news of this martyrdom had a particular affect on me since I was a peer of all of those who died. The Lord used their experience to motivate me to serious thinking concerning my own usefulness in missionary endeavor. It is obvious when God takes some home and leaves others, those who are left must think through the ramifications of that. I did, and God used it in my life."

Dave Howard, Jim Elliot's brother-in-law, served

with the Latin America Mission and as missionary director for Intervarsity Christian Fellowship before becoming director of the Consultation on World Evangelism held in Thailand in June 1980: "I can't quote any statistics, but I can say that everywhere I go I continue to run into people whose lives were touched because of Palm Beach or because of the writings about the five martyrs and the Aucas. Among college students today I don't know of any book that has had a greater influence than Jim's biography, *Shadow of the Almighty*, which my sister put together from his journals.

"There is one incident from my travels that particularly sticks with me. In 1959 I was in Colombia as a missionary and visiting a remote spot where an exciting new church had sprung up. I had to travel by bus, jeep, river launch, dugout canoe, and finally by foot to get to this place back on the backside of nowhere. I spent a day or two with the eager, zealous young Colombian preacher and in our conversation naturally asked, 'How'd you get into God's work? How'd you get way out here?' This is what he said: 'I was a shoemaker. I don't know if you ever heard about it or not, but five American missionaries were killed in Ecuador about three years ago. When I heard about how they had given their lives, I told the Lord I would give up my shoemaking business and somehow replace at least one; so I came out here where the gospel had never been proclaimed.' When I told him about my relationship with the five, he was utterly astounded. 'I never thought I would meet anybody who knew any of those martyrs,' he said, 'but their deaths changed my life.' "

*"We call them martyrs. But you know what the
Bible calls them? Witnesses. The word for
witness is marturia. So in God's categories it
really doesn't matter whether, humanly
speaking, you win or lose, whether you're a
victim or a victor. You're a witness."*
Elisabeth Elliot

The Families Today 13

The Palm Beach martyrs left five widows and nine children, a legacy that cannot be measured in terms of material wealth. We have followed these families at intervals as they scattered and took various paths in life. Today, all but one of the widows are in their fifties, and two are grandmothers. The youngest child, Matthew McCully, just turned twenty-five; the oldest is thirty-two. Each received several thousand dollars from the fund established by Dr. Edman, Clyde Taylor, and General Harrison. Seven of the nine completed college.

We again pick up the threads of the lives of these and their families who will always have a special place in the hearts of millions of evangelicals in this era and beyond. Where are they now? How have they been influenced by the memory of their loved ones and the massacre in which they died? We will look at each family in the light of our interviews with all the widows and some of the children.

Olive Fleming Liefeld, the youngest of the widows, lives with her seminary professor husband, Walter, and their three children in a red brick, split-level house near the campus of the Trinity Evangelical Divinity School in

Deerfield, Illinois. Their oldest, David, is an engineering major at the University of Illinois. Beverly, eighteen, completed high school in 1980 and was accepted at Wheaton College. Holly, twelve, is in the sixth grade. "From time to time, each of our children has asked questions about what happened in Ecuador," Walt observes. "They've heard the stories at church and at Christian camp. They say to themselves, *That's my mom!*"

Olive still receives invitations to speak about the experience; she accepts them if possible. "Sometimes weeks go by without my thinking of it," she says. "Sometimes, when I do, it seems like a dream."

She has never felt bitterness or resentment, "mainly because I feel God really prepared me. Pete had kept a diary while he was single in Ecuador, and I was reading it just before Palm Beach. Several times he wrote that he would be willing to give his life for the Aucas, and I questioned him about it. He didn't feel that God was going to require that for the Aucas, but it never left my thinking."

"That was one reason I wanted to meet Olive," Walt recalls. "From what I had heard of her, I sensed that here was someone in whose life God had worked most uniquely, and that God must know what kind of person she was to allow her to go through this."

The aura that many evangelicals still place around his wife has never bothered Walt. "Here's a funny incident. After we were married, we went to a church where I was to speak and were introduced as 'Olive Fleming and husband.' I told Olive that I felt like the queen of England's husband, Prince Philip.

"Actually, her experience has been a tremendous help to us. It's been part of the glue in our marriage. We are always conscious of her, not just as a wife but as somebody chosen by God for a remarkable experience. We feel that we are partners in anything we do."

Walt, the theologian, and Olive, the former missionary, have both reflected a great deal on the Palm Beach killings.

"I've heard people say that God put Pete and his friends there to be killed," Olive says. "I've never believed that for one minute. We don't have to vindicate God, to say why God did this. It is enough for me to know that He took the circumstances and used them for His glory in front of the world."

"Death is always an enemy," Walt notes. "Paul said the last enemy to be destroyed is death. But God can use death and does indeed permit death for His purposes. But we have to be careful lest we say, 'God did this for this purpose.' We need to be very sensitive about that, humble ourselves, and give God time to work out His purposes.

"We realize it won't be until eternity that we'll really know why God chose to allow it to happen. It makes me very cautious before I pontificate as to why God allowed this or that. I confess it has also made me very careful in talking with people who have been bereaved, because I have learned so much from Olive as to her reaction. It has made me very, very careful as I have tried to help other people."

Marilou McCully has now lived in suburban Seattle and worked in the administrative offices of Auburn Hospital for seventeen years. She considered remarriage a couple of times but only once seriously. Her suitors were single fellows with no experience with raising children. "I just couldn't see either as the father of my sons." Her eyes still light up for Ed, as anyone can plainly see.

Raising three active, sports-minded sons, Marilou has

had her good times and hard times. "I haven't had much time for leisure," she admits, "but we've had lots of fun. The boys brought their friends home and played field hockey outside by the hour. With kids running in and out, there was never a dull moment."

When Mike, her middle son, was in the first grade, he was found to be suffering from a disintegrating femur. For a year and a half he had to wear a brace on that leg and be very careful. The problem didn't prevent him from playing high-school sports and developing into a rugged outdoor man. The only son who is single, Mike now travels the country, training thoroughbred horses.

Steve, who was the same age in 1980 as his father when he was killed, was discovered to be diabetic at fifteen. "It seems I spent my whole life cooking special things for him," Marilou recalls. "He served as captain of his high-school football team and became a teacher-coach. Fortunately, he married a home-ec major, who is also a teacher."

Matt, who married before Steve, most resembles Ed. His basketball team at the University of Puget Sound won the small-college championship in 1976. He is now a sportswriter for a newspaper in eastern Washington.

With her boys out of the nest, Marilou has moved to a condominium nearer her work. She sees Steve regularly, Matt a little less, and Mike once or twice a year. Ed's sister, Peg, brother Jay, and their widowed mother, Lois, live a few miles away. Marilou also stays in touch with her family in Michigan.

Her brother-in-law, Bill Erickson and Dr. Jay McCully, have been more than uncles to her three boys. "If one of my sons had a problem and wanted to talk to a man, Bill or Jay was always available. Jay, who is an elder in the Plymouth Brethren church we attended when the boys were growing up, married Steve.

"Our three families were very close, eating together on special occasions, attending the games of children, helping one another out when needed. When my boys were small, I would drop them off at school. They'd catch the bus home to Peg's, and she took care of them until I got home. Often she had dinner fixed before I got there. I don't know what I'd have done without Peg. She was like a second mother to my boys."

Marilou's father-in-law went to heaven over a decade ago. After his death, Grandma McCully joined her children and grandchildren in Seattle. Now in her eighties, this dignified, silver-haired lady stands tall and straight and takes care of herself nicely in the mother-in-law apartment she occupies at Peg's and Bill's. She is a joy to all three families.

The only other surviving parent of the Palm Beach martyrs, Clara Elliot, still lives in the family home in Portland, Oregon. Jim's father died in 1970, at eighty-three. His picture beams from the living room mantel, a picture taken at a picnic a week before he died. He spent his last years showing a slide presentation to churches and other interested groups of the story told in *Through Gates of Splendor*. On the other end of the mantel is a pencil sketch of Jim that was used on one of the Auca books.

After arthritis forced her to give up chiropractic practice, Mrs. Elliot turned to a correspondence and prayer ministry with missionaries. Her hands are now so crippled that she can hardly write a letter, but she keeps trying and does her own housework and cooking, too. A brother-in-law looks in on her every day and sees that she gets to Brethren services on Sunday. Through Brethren contacts, she keeps up with the McCullys in Seattle, and they with her.

Although Marilou has not been back to Ecuador for

almost seventeen years, she's continually reminded of her past. People come up to her and ask, "Wasn't your husband one of the five missionaries killed by the Aucas?"

She smiles and says "Yes," but she now rarely takes speaking engagements.

She acknowledges that the results of the sacrifice of the five have been gratifying. "We want to judge what God did by that. We want to say that the death of the five men was God's way to reach the Aucas and to send a lot of Americans to the mission field. But we haven't any idea of why God allowed them to be killed. We should leave that mystery to Him."

Marilou's dear friend Barbara Youderian has remained in Ecuador, where she continues as manager of the GMU guest house in Quito. Her guest bedrooms are usually full of missionaries coming into the capital on business or to see their children during the school year; other guests are friends of the mission visiting from the United States and Canada. "I've learned a lot about serving since I came to the mission field," she says. "I never thought I'd be in a guest home. But just being here, realizing that missionaries are human, and being sensitive to their needs and problems has been a joyous opportunity for service."

Barbara attends the English Fellowship Church in Quito, teaches a home Bible class for English-speaking women, and participates in a women's fellowship group. "Our group has craft classes, slumber parties, and lots of other fun things. I don't have time to feel sorry for myself or to do all the things I want to do."

Her children are also on their own. Beth, now twenty-eight, was married in June 1978 in Milwaukee, and Barbara went north for the wedding. "It's marvelous how the Lord took care of Beth, leading her through nurse's training and directing her to the Brethren chapel in Milwaukee, where she met her future husband. Beth didn't know, when she went there, that this was the assembly to which Ed McCully had belonged. So the Lord provided her with special friends."

Barbara's son, Jerry, twenty-six, is still single. After schooling in Ecuador, he attended the Bible Institute of Los Angeles and California State University as a business major. Now an auditor for the Bank of America, he is involved with the First Evangelical Free Church of Fullerton, California, where Charles Swindoll is pastor.

Barbara has no regrets about Operation Auca. "God was there, just as He was with us after we learned the men were killed. He was working out His perfect will, which we'll understand fully some day."

Heaven is more precious to Barbara now. "I want to see the Lord first, and Rog, of course. But my parents are there also and so many dear friends with the Lord. I'm looking forward to a joyful reunion."

Marj Saint Van Der Puy has much the same philosophy as her neighbor about keeping busy. "The worst thing you can do is sit around and feel sorry for yourself. As a Christian, I don't think you have any right to. When we consider what the Lord has done for us, what can we do that has any comparison?"

Marj has now spent thirty-two years of her life as a missionary, including about three years' furlough time in the United States. Her second husband, Abe Van Der Puy, is president of World Radio Missionary Fellowship, which includes HCJB, the missionary speaker for the "Back to the Bible" radio broadcast, and a leading figure worldwide in evangelical missionary circles. Marj works in various HCJB offices, serves on committees, helps with hospitality, and keeps their house running. "I do everything I can to free Abe for the jobs the

Lord gave him, to leave him free for the larger tasks."

Looking back almost a quarter century, she wouldn't say Palm Beach "changed the direction of my life. It just confirmed the direction in which I was already going, made me want to be sure of my priorities, made me see the difference between the trivial and the important as never before."

Marj has spoken about the experience hundreds of times and written even more letters to inquirers about the martyrdom and happenings among the Aucas. Piles of letters, she says, still come to HCJB from every continent, asking what has happened since. Wherever she and Abe go, they meet people who say their lives were changed by what happened to the five missionaries.

She is not one to doubt or to indulge in theological debate about the why or wherefore of the incident. Her faith is straightforward and certain. "I don't think that God is ever the author of anything that is not for our ultimate good. I had no trouble believing that the night they told us the fellows were dead. I had known those fellows—one was my husband—and had prayed with them in our home. I knew that step by step they had looked for the Lord's will. I could only believe that this was the next step."

Marj's three children are married, and she is a grandmother. Philip, the youngest, is wed to a pastor's daughter he met at Trinity College in Deerfield, Illinois. Both teach at a Christian school in Wilmar, Minnesota, where older brother, Steve, is a residential land developer and builder. Steve is on the school board and is married to a local girl whom he met when she came to Ecuador with a church choral group. Steve and his wife, Ginny, have three of Marj's grandchildren, Shaun, Jamie, and Jessie. Their sister, Kathy, is the only missionary among the nine children left fatherless by the

Auca massacre. In 1972 she became a "drowned Saint" (her words) as the bride of Ross Drown, son of the missionary who led the ground rescue team to search for the bodies of the five martyrs. Kathy and Ross and their two boys, Daren and Brent, serve with MAF in Honduras. Philip and Steve are also pilots. Marj's children refer to their father as Dad Nate and their stepfather as Dad Abe.

Phil Saint was just eleven days past his first birthday at the time of the massacre and cannot remember his father. Steve, who retains his father's blond hair, was five and can still remember standing on the mound in the yard and watching Dad Nate take off. Steve also has memories of his birthday twenty-two days after his father was killed. "I can remember asking if the moon was a hole in heaven and if the spots were my father and God looking down on us."

The influence of Nate Saint and the Auca incident is stamped heavily on his three children. All are strong, committed Christians and feel close to their father, whose voice is on the film, "Conquering Jungle Barriers," that was made for MAF before his death. "I have a letter," Steve says, "that Dad wrote to his younger brother Ben about choosing a life partner and what is involved in marriage. I can just feel that I had written it. Dad Nate's influence is all over me, and influence from the Aucas as well. I've felt all my life that an easy Christianity is to be questioned. It's free to get, but once you have it, it carries responsibility."

The Saint boys attended schools in the United States. Kathy went first to Capernway Bible School in England, where the book *Jungle Pilot* "really had an impact on me. I sort of read the book as though it weren't about my father. I wanted to know what made this man Nate Saint love the Lord as he did. It challenged me in the same way it has challenged many people. I think Dad Nate and Mom's generation knew something about the Lord that we don't."

Attaining her degree in education from Northern Illinois University, Kathy became reacquainted with Ross Drown while she was teaching and he was attending Trinity College. They had been schoolmates for a couple of years in Quito.

They joined MAF after Ross received his degree. "I never felt that I was particularly called to the mission field. I think you should ask yourself, 'Am I not called,' rather than, 'Am I?' because there is such a need in third-world countries."

Kathy is helpmeet to her husband in Honduras, just as her mother helped her father at Shell Mera. And Kathy's two children run out to see their daddy take off.

"Mom always told me, 'Prepare to be a widow. Be thinking in your mind of the possibility of giving him up. Be able to handle things alone.' I was raised with that in mind."

Kathy remembers a time when she was at a small jungle hospital in southern Mexico, awaiting the birth of their first child while Ross was ferrying Wycliffe trainees to their jungle training camp. "I heard one of the MAF pilots say, 'There has been an accident. Ross has gone down.' That's all I knew until I heard that the plane had set down in a pile of sleeping bags and duffle bags. He wasn't hurt at all."

What if she should suffer the loss of her young husband? "It would be hard, but I'd accept it. I think that's what happened with Mom when Dad Nate died. She accepted it as being within God's will. Her peace passed on to us. I would hope that same peace would pass to my children."

"One of America's most admired Christian women"

is how one publisher promotes the best-known of the widows of the Palm Beach massacre. Her old friends still call her Betty, but she now prefers Elisabeth, the name she has always used on her books. The title of one of her newest books, *Love Has A Price Tag*, is hardly an exaggeration.

Not that she pleases everybody. Christian feminists don't appreciate her published views that men should hold authority in the church. They were flustered when she came to one of their conferences in Washington. "They didn't invite me to speak, but I made some comments in workshops and in open discussions on the floor. They said I was a confusing role model. I don't fit their pattern. A woman who is visible and articulate is not supposed to be a nonfeminist."

Her books have aroused controversy because "I do not write to please people, but God." About *No Graven Image*, which portrayed the disappointment and disillusionment of her character, Margaret Sparhawk, on the mission field, she says, "I was trying to say something about who God is, to get at the basis of faith: Do you trust God for who He is or for what He is supposed to do? Like leaving John the Baptist in prison to have his head chopped off. Would God ever do things like that? Would He let five men who trusted Him get speared? The problem is we don't know God. If we really know Him, we don't try to put Him in a box or defend Him. It's a question of authority. Are we really under His authority?"

Those who believe Israel can do no wrong did not appreciate her *Furnace of the Lord*. Harper & Row sent her to Israel after the Six Day War in 1967 to see if the Israeli victory over the Arabs had resulted in a "new Jerusalem." She concluded it hadn't and indicated her doubts about the godliness of Israel. Zionism, she said, was "a purely political movement with no religious purpose, a point generally overlooked by those who see in it a kind of return to God."

"My editor," she recalls, "told me I had handled a delicate subject most indelicately and asked that I see another publisher." Doubleday did the book and, according to an editor, received a barrage of complaints.

A Christian publisher once wanted to send her to Indonesia to do a book about miracles, including resurrections from the dead, reported to have occurred there in a great Christian awakening. " 'What if I go down there and find these miracles are not true?' I asked. 'Could I put that in the book?' The publisher replied, 'Well, we won't have trouble publishing the facts, but we might have problems publishing your interpretations of the facts.' 'Well,' I said, 'if you are asking me to write a book, you are asking me to interpret the facts, aren't you?' They said, 'You'll hear from us.' I never heard another thing."

Elisabeth Elliot speaks to a wide variety of audiences: women's retreats; conventions; colleges; seminaries; and the biennial Intervarsity missionary conference, where she has become a regular. She speaks on missions, the private life of a disciple, suffering, the mystery of sexuality, and many other subjects. Audiences find her disturbing but seldom dull. She would be the last to call herself a *popular* speaker.

She may be most respected as a speaker on suffering; for as one admirer, Harold Myra, publisher of *Christianity Today*, puts it: "We know she's been there." Her testing shows when she says, "Almost everything in the Bible is the reverse of what the world says. As Paul defines it, in our weaknesses we learn to know His strength. In an experience of loss, of coming to the end of one's self, you become aware that God does provide all that you need. All."

Myra calls her "one of the few really quality Christian writers and speakers of our day. Great writers," he says, "are usually developed through a lot of suffering. She's been thrown into the fire, where she had no choice but to face it."

He refers to the fact that she's lost not one husband but two. Her second husband, Addison Leitch, died of cancer in 1974—"a gradual disintegration," she recalls sadly. After his death, she decided to take in student lodgers from nearby Gordon-Conwell Theological Seminary, where Addison had taught and she served as a visiting professor of missions. The first two lodgers became her son-in-law and third husband.

Her daughter, Valerie, was then a student at Wheaton College. "She never felt any pressure there because of who her father was," Elisabeth says. "She was proud to be the daughter of Jim Elliot." The younger boarder, Presbyterian divinity student Walter Shepard, married Valerie. They live today in Laurel, Mississippi, where he is pastor of Trinity Presbyterian Church. The older lodger, Lars Gren, a former salesman, was married to Elisabeth four years after Addison Leitch's death.

Lars and Elisabeth lived in Atlanta a short time while he was a chaplain at the Milledgeville State Hospital. Today they are back in a northern Boston suburb. Lars, a big, muscular man ("I go for the strong ones," Elisabeth says with a laugh), serves as his wife's manager and agent, travels with her, and handles the sales of her books. He is also an assistant in managing a private foundation.

In public, she prefers her first husband's name, "for that's what people know and remember me by"; in private, she is Mrs. Lars Gren, indicating her preference

for the traditional marriage relationship. She has many
fond remembrances of both her deceased husbands and
doesn't mind saying so. Jim Elliot's picture hangs on
her living-room wall. "He still seems real to me. I continue to dream about him occasionally."

She constantly meets people who have made a commitment because of the Auca massacre. One is a missionary priest from the Episcopal church she attends.
"We call him the Flying Priest of Labrador. His reason
for becoming a missionary was the death of the five
men."

She has good memories of the Aucas and says she
"learned lots from them. I determined to raise Valerie
the way they raised their children. My son-in-law told
me recently that he never ceases to be amazed at Valerie's patience under trying circumstances. I told him
she learned that from the Aucas."

Elisabeth last visited the Aucas in 1976, arriving the
day after Rachel left to seek medical treatment for her
eyes. "They all wore clothes and looked bedraggled."
Then tongue-in-cheek she says, "There's nothing like
ruining naked Indians by putting clothes on them."

Listening to her reminisce, one receives the impression that she has forgotten few details of her years in
Ecuador. She speaks warmly of Quichua and Auca
friends, of her fellow widows and many other missionaries. Yet she does not deny the conflicts of the
past, nor does she object to some of these problems
being aired.

"Who does it help to know about the division between Paul and Barnabas?" Elizabeth continues.
"About David committing adultery with Bathsheba?
Everybody! Because it demonstrates that where sin
abounded, grace did much more abound. How can we
appreciate grace if we don't face the sin? I've been a

controversial figure simply because I have tried to tell the truth as I see it. It is not necessarily palatable.

"Only God knows whether my motives are pure. God knows I am a sinner. God also knows that my vision is limited. I can't see the whole truth about anything. Neither can Rachel. But what I am responsible for is what I do see. If I see a thing, I am not going to back down."

When the question comes up about why the five men died (a question she has been asked "more times than I wish to remember"), her eyes flash in obvious consternation. "Any answer you try to give is extremely limited and naive because the purposes of God are inscrutable. I have strenuously objected to what I consider glib and superficial attempts to say the reasons are a, b, and c—that God did this for the salvation of the Aucas or any other reason.

"The editorializing in Christian papers following the killings, I found very upsetting. I could understand secular papers saying 'Why didn't the blankety-blank fools keep out of there.' That's human reasoning. That makes sense, if you don't happen to believe in the sovereignty of God. But the glib and often superficial attempts by Christians to *explain* their death in terms of the salvation of the Aucas, the calling of others to the mission field, or for any other reason—this I found upsetting.

"Certainly God is interested in the salvation of the Aucas. He's interested in *anyone's* salvation. I don't think He is more interested in their salvation than in others. It seems to me presumptuous to say that because these men died, God has got to vindicate Himself by a number of people being saved or a number being called to the mission field.

"I have always believed, and I still believe, and I have

said this a hundred times—God knew exactly what He was doing. God was in charge. Romans 8:28: Everything fits in a pattern for our good. If part of that pattern happens to be visible and understandable to us, like the salvation of a certain number of Aucas or the calling of missionaries, fine. Thank God.

"If God never saved an Auca and He never called anyone to the mission field, I would still have no question in my mind that the death of these men was a part of His pattern for good.

"I've never changed from that belief. I've hung my soul on the sovereignty of God. That is the bedrock of my belief."

And that is also the belief of Marilou, Marj, Barbara, Olive, and thousands of other Christians who will never be the same because of what happened on an Ecuadorian jungle beach on January 8, 1956.

Afterword

We followed developments in the Auca story from the first reports on the disappearance of the five missionaries. Over the years, we wrote a number of articles based on interviews with Rachel Saint, Uncle Cam Townsend, and other Wycliffe personnel. We were the only journalists to interview Kimo and Komi as they were passing through the United States on their way home from Berlin. At that time, Kimo invited us to visit his people. "I promise, we won't spear you," he said, with Rachel interpreting.

When we began to write this book, we thought we were well-grounded in the happenings since 1956. The research turned out to take far more time than we had anticipated. There always seemed to be one more person to interview, one more telephone call to make, one more fact to check. Even now more could be done.

None of our sources, who include all the living principals in the Auca story, should be blamed for unintentional errors and faulty interpretations. Nor should this book be perceived as having the endorsement of any individual or organization. We are aware that certain conflicts may come as a surprise to some readers. We all know that among Christians, as well as other human beings, conflicts are inevitable. We have simply endeavored to fulfill our responsibility as journalists and historians in telling the story of the five martyrs and succeeding events among the Aucas. We believe we can best honor God by including all sides and trying to be fair to all parties in disputes that may have arisen while trying to fulfill God's commands.

Closer to home, we wish to thank our daughter, Cheri, who also made the trip to Ecuador, took pictures, and made supplementary notes; our neighbor and friend Fay Parks, who typed the manuscript, finishing at 2:30 A.M. one Saturday morning; and our Canadian friend Don Rhodes, a budding young linguistic scholar, for carefully proofreading the final text.

Elisabeth Elliot

No Graven Image

Foreword by J. I. Packer

'Dynamite. . . I first read *No Graven Image* ten years ago, and it bowled me over; partly, no doubt, because its vision of God struck so many chords in my own experience. I thought it was a little classic; I count myself honoured to be asked to commend it to a new generation of readers, and I do so with very great pleasure.'

J. I. Packer

'Mrs Elliot has drawn upon her experience of South America, of missionary life, of faith under trial, to produce a novel which is more than competent, which hauntingly asks some searching questions, and hints at a possible answer.'

Crusade

26355 5

£1.95

Elisabeth Elliot

The Mark Of A Man

"The world cries out for men who are strong — strong in conviction, strong to lead, to stand, to suffer. I pray that you will be that kind of man, Pete, glad that God made you a man, glad to shoulder the burden of manliness. . ."

In *Let Me Be A Woman*, written as a wedding gift for her daughter Valerie, the author praised what she called the 'divinely ordained' role of women. Here she voices similar strong convictions — to her nephew Pete — about what it means to be a man.

We only have to look at Jesus' own life, she says, to find out what true masculinity is all about. The acceptance of responsibility, sacrifice, forgiveness, suffering and courage were made visible in His life on earth. The man who follows Him must take the same path.

Elisabeth Elliot was wife to Jim Elliot, one of the missionaries murdered in Ecuador by the Auca Indians.

27566 9

£1.95

Judy Wurmbrand

Escape From The Grip

A Jewish girl's discovery of Christ and freedom

This is the autobiography of a young Romanian Jewish
girl. In Judy the spark of freedom will not be extinguished.
She learns early in life how to survive and preserve her
identity under an all-prevading dictatorship, in the shadow
of the secret police. At last, her family find a way to leave
the country they had loved.
To a great extent all is triggered off by her childhood
neighbour, Michael Wurmbrand (son of the legendary
Pastor Richard Wurmbrand, fourteen years imprisoned for
his faith). Years later, while in Israel, separated from him,
she embraces the Christain faith and later marries
Michael. They now live in the States.

27150 7   £1.75